75+
READING
STRATEGIES

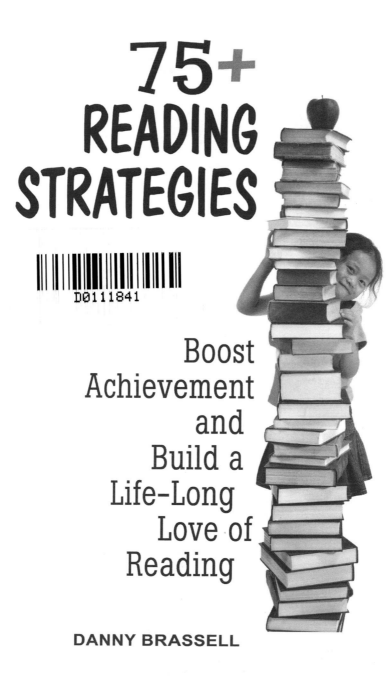

‖‖‖‖‖‖‖‖‖‖‖‖‖‖‖
D0111841

Boost
Achievement
and
Build a
Life-Long
Love of
Reading

DANNY BRASSELL

Crystal Springs
SDE BOOKS

a division of Staff Development for Educators
Peterborough, New Hampshire

Published by Crystal Springs Books
A division of Staff Development for Educators (SDE)
10 Sharon Road, PO Box 500
Peterborough, NH 03458
1-800-321-0401
www.sde.com/crystalsprings

©2009 Crystal Springs Books
Illustrations ©2009 Crystal Springs Books

Published 2009
Printed in the United States of America
13 12 11 10 09   1 2 3 4 5

ISBN: 978-1-934026-95-3

Library of Congress Cataloging-in-Publication Data

Brassell, Danny.
  75+ reading strategies : boost achievement & build a life-long love of reading / Danny
    Brassell.
    p. cm.
  Includes bibliographical references and index.
  ISBN 978-1-934026-95-3
  1. Reading (Elementary) 2. Children--Books and reading. 3. Motivation in education.
      I. Title. II. Title: Seventy-five plus reading strategies.
  LB1573.B6927 2009
  372.41--dc22
                          2009023312

Editor: Roberta Bell
Art Director and Designer: Soosen Dunholter
Production Coordinator: Deborah Fredericks
Illustrations:
Joyce Rainville pages: 15, 17, 52, 56, 58, 66, 69, 106, 116, 125
Phyllis Pittet pages: 26, 30, 33, 34, 41, 62, 114
Patrick Belfiori: page 51

This book is dedicated to all of my friends at SDE.

Contents

CHAPTER 2: TALK 40

CHAPTER 3: CLASS SYSTEMS 64

Acknowledgments

What most people do not seem to understand about publishing is that while any author may enjoy his or her name on a book's spine, no work could possibly be the effort of any single individual.

This book exists because of Kendra Fowler. Period. She is my cheerleader, and I greatly value all that she does on my behalf. Roberta Bell has made me appear literate by encouraging me to constantly make my writing as clear as possible and adding her own flavors to "spice-up" my writing. Sharon Smith, who has helped me before as an editor, continues to be patient and positive with me, and I am grateful.

I have had the pleasure to speak for a number of organizations, and there is none finer than SDE. It has stuck with me through thick and thin, and I marvel at the quality of presenters and support staff that it attracts. Jim Grant created a dandy of a company that provides superior professional development opportunities for teachers. I am indebted to nearly everyone at SDE in some way, but the two people in the conferences and customized training divisions that I'd like to especially thank in print are Liz LaRoche and Mark Bemont. These two superheroes coordinate my travel arrangements and those of hundreds of other employees, and they make my life easier in countless ways.

My family deserves so much credit for putting up with Daddy's travel away from home. I have a gorgeous wife, Jeanie, who has blessed me with the world's three greatest children: Kate (now five years old), Sean (now four years old), and baby Samantha (now three weeks old). I love all of you, and please know that I am working hard to be home more frequently. On the road, you are all in my thoughts and prayers.

Finally, because this is a book of reading strategies, I would be remiss not to thank colleagues and mentors who have helped shape my thoughts and beliefs: Stephen Krashen, Robert Rueda, David Yaden, Diane Lapp, Doug Fisher, Nancy Frey, Jim Trelease, and Tim Rasinski. Keep on offering teachers your expertise and support, and thank you for all of your encouragement in my professional life.

Introduction

Over the years I have come across a number of definitions of reading, but none ever satisfied me like those from students. Here are some definitions offered by first, second, and third graders with whom I studied:

—"Reading is what you do when there ain't a movie about it." (DeSean, age 6)

— "Reading is something my mom tells me I need to do." (Courtney, age 7)

— "Reading is when I go to the library with my mom and she sits me on her lap and we cuddle and giggle." (Jacob, age 6)

— "Reading is saying the words fast and getting a treasure box ticket." (Kyara, age 7)

— "Reading is boring." (Victor, age 8)

Do your students moan when they hear it's time to read? Do they read only to earn stickers or pizza parties? How do you entice students to read for fun on their own?

You're in luck. Reading is my passion. I love inspiring students to read, and I know a ton about reluctant and struggling readers. Why? I was one. I learned a long time ago that the best way to get people to do anything is to make it fun and make them think they thought of it.

Whenever I began a reading class, we would start with a number of chants. So now you chant with me:

Welcome

This is the class –

Who wants to learn –

And read more books –

And make a better tomorrow!

Now, this next chant requires that you understand some words in Spanish, so I will teach you those words. The first word is *sí*, so please repeat *sí*. Great. *Sí* means "yes." Now the second word is *libros*. Say *libros*. That means "books." So answer my queries:

Bienvenidos

¿Quieres aprender? (Do you want to learn?) *¡Sí!*

¿Quieres aventura? (Do you want adventure?) *¡Sí!*

¿Quieres leer? (Do you want to read?) *¡Sí!*

¿Qué tienen información? (What has information?) *¡Libros!*

¿Qué tienen fotos bonitos? (What has pretty pictures?) *¡Libros!*

¿Qué tienen cuentos? (What has stories?) *¡Libros!*

Great! So now we shout together:

2, 4, 6, 8 –

What do we appreciate?

Reading.

Reading!

Yeah!

Are you ready to have fun? I used to always ask my young students that, and they would shout, "Yeah." "Good," I'd reply, "because today we're going to have lots of fun!" I have been training teachers at various universities for over 10 years, and not once has one of my bosses come into my office and said, "Danny, today we're going to have some fun," but I love starting the day off with a lot of positive energy. And that is what I want you to take from this book. Love your job. Love your kids. Love reading.

My purpose for this book is to give you all sorts of tricks, ideas—strategies—that will make you a better reading teacher. My goal is that you finish this book feeling like a <u>R</u>isk-taking, <u>E</u>xcited, <u>A</u>nd <u>D</u>etermined <u>E</u>ducator <u>R</u>eaching <u>S</u>tudents. Hey, that spells out "readers." Pretty clever, huh? My objective is that you get at least 75 reading strategies from this book, but you may get even more. What I mean by that is that if you are like me, the best part about listening to other folks describe their teaching ideas is that their ideas usually help me come up with new ones of my own, as well. I also love putting new spins on old ideas.

Raise your hand if you remember exactly how you learned to read.

Raise your hand if you like to read.

You need to know that learning to read is like learning to ride a bike: it becomes easier with experience. We know that experience leads to confidence, and confidence with any activity leads to much more practice of that activity. Well, that sounds simple enough. People might even say, "that's easy." But anything is easy once you know how to do it. It's the "getting to know how to do it" that's difficult. It is often difficult for adults to understand the frustrations children feel when learning to read because most adults cannot remember what it was like before they knew how to read.

So what's the problem? Well, there are actually two conditions to consider. There is a condition known as "illiteracy," which means you do not know how to read, and there's a condition called "alliteracy," which means you choose not to read. Both are paralyzing, but I'd like to argue that there is no such thing as illiteracy, only alliteracy. Children are choosing not to read.

Look at all of the media competing for children's attention nowadays. There are movies and television shows with such rapid cuts that it's no wonder children have attention deficit disorder. Kids can open 15 windows on the Internet at once. And there are some video games with characters that look more human than some of the celebrities I see in Hollywood. Kids are ignoring books in droves, and our job is to reintroduce students to the pleasures of reading.

I have asked thousands of people how they learned to read. Not once has somebody told me, "Well, when I was young, my grandmother would sit me on her lap. We sat in a special rocking chair together. And Grandma would point to the words and say 'a-a-alligator….b-b-ball.' "

Would you like to know the secret to teaching reading? Close the door, and do not share this information with anyone else (unless they buy this book): reading should always be fun. Human beings are pleasure-oriented creatures. I'll give you an example. A few months ago, my wife and I were finishing dinner when Jeanie asked, "Would you like more green beans, honey?" After I shook my head "no" and told her I was stuffed, she mentioned that we had apple pie for dessert. "Just a small slice," I said.

Have you ever noticed that you find room for the activities you enjoy? Our goal is to make kids love reading. You know you're having an impact when the recess bell rings, and students do not leave their desks because they are more concerned about finishing whatever chapter they're on.

Keep in mind that every student is different. What works for Ephraim does not necessarily work for Niceysha. Remember that there is no single approach that works with every child. Over the years, I've had to adapt my teaching style to encourage struggling students and English language learners, as well as my gifted students.

Every classroom contains a huge range of abilities. For example, if you teach second grade, you are not teaching just second grade. You are teaching anywhere from fifth grade to preschool. Every class I have ever taught has some students who arrive at school early, know all their times tables and state capitals, and finish half an hour earlier than their classmates on just about every assignment. And every class I have taught has students who show up 10 minutes late to class every day, don't even know how to hold their pencils, and manage to promptly forget what was learned on Monday by Tuesday morning. Every student requires his own strategies, and this is one of the greatest challenges and joys of teaching.

Throughout this book, I share a plethora of strategies I have used with students of all ages and abilities to get them excited about reading. Call them tricks of the trade, great ideas—whatever you want. Just make sure you take whatever you like and share it with your students. As you read, please consider one simple question that I always ask the teachers I train to consider: what good is teaching students *how* to read if they never *want* to read? By the time you finish this book, I hope you will be excited about reading and fuel the fire that lights a community of avid readers in your classroom.

CHAPTER 1

Environment

I worked for a while in the restaurant industry. By that I mean that for several summers, I worked as a "Sandwich Board Man" in my hometown of Durango, Colorado. I wore a 35-pound aluminum-framed sandwich board that fit on me like a tortoise shell, and I walked back and forth along Main Avenue between the old train depot on 5th Street and Old Tymer's Café on 10th Street, recommending restaurants to tourists. "When referring people to restaurants," my boss told me, "keep in mind that surveys show that customers consider the quality of food to be the third most important trait of any good restaurant. Number two is quality of service, and most important to customers is the atmosphere and the ambience." So basically, restaurants can cook customers horrible meals as long as they deliver the meals promptly with a smile in a nice environment.

Teachers need to consider the reading environments they create. I do not think teachers should slack on the quality of their lessons or the content they offer students, mind you. I do believe, though, that great reading teachers create classroom environments that constantly inspire students to want to read. A good reading environment should encourage students to do as much reading as possible. Whenever students choose to read without the teacher telling them to do so, that teacher is creating a positive classroom reading environment. Remember: you don't have to spend a lot of money to create a wonderful classroom reading environment.

1 Environmental Print

The thing I like the most about environmental print is that no matter where you live you can find a variety of items to read. I have always taught in under-resourced areas where students may not have access to lots of books or magazines at home. This is a major cause of concern, as research has shown that students with limited reading resources in the home do much more poorly in school than those who have lots of books at home. However, billboards, candy wrappers, soup can labels, and a host of other printed materials surround us every day, and teachers can encourage students to pay close attention to the print around them.

I used environmental print all the time because I also don't believe teachers should spend a lot of their own money on their classrooms. By encouraging students to bring in shoe boxes and milk cartons and cereal boxes and the like, teachers can show students how to read the print on daily items and even make games from these items. For example,

take an empty cereal box a student will have brought to class and cut small slits along the sides of the first letter in the name of the cereal. Then create a "ticker tape" with all 26 letters of the alphabet for students to slide where that letter had been. Cut slits in the sides of the box as well so you can pull the tape from side to side. Students then read aloud the new word created.

I did this exercise with an empty Cheerios box, and my students loved it.

"Beerios…Deerios…Feerios," Carlos giggled. "Oh my gosh! This is the greatest game of my life!"

Not only have you created a fun phonemic awareness activity, you have also demonstrated to students how to recycle, create thinking games from easily accessible items, and pay closer attention to print they encounter.

2 Make Time to Read

This is my Sally Struthers speech: in 10 minutes a day—the time it takes to drink a cup of coffee—you could have a tremendous impact on students' reading ability. Here is why I emphasize this so much. In all my years of teaching, I have learned that no matter what I do, I cannot control my students' home environments. I can, however, influence my classroom environment. There is not a single K–12 teacher in America who can tell me she cannot find 10 minutes a day for students to read on their own. Heck, if you teach grades 1–3 you should be able to find at least 30 minutes each day for students to read.

I used to use reading as a way to calm my students. Sure, students who finished their other work early were always encouraged to read, but all students had a chance to read for 7 to 10 minutes after our morning recess, lunch break, and afternoon recess. We always played music during reading (by the way, let the kids choose the music, and after about three weeks of choosing hip hop and popular music they will start selecting instrumental pieces like jazz, classical, and nature music). I allowed students to read wherever they wanted with whomever they wanted, and they could eat and drink. Again, my objective is to make kids love reading.

The research is pretty clear on this point. It does not matter what you read; all that matters is how much you read. It does not matter if you are reading James Joyce or *James and the Giant Peach*. People who read more, read better. I am on an airplane at least once a week, and I cannot remember the last time I sat next to someone who was reading something by Molière or Dostoyevsky or Shakespeare. I can always find seats cluttered with passengers engrossed, however, by *USA Today*, *People* magazine, or a Danielle Steel novel.

I know that the more I can encourage my students to read for fun in a comfortable environment, the more likely my students are to associate reading with pleasure. If I can get my kids to like reading, there is a greater chance my students will choose to read on their own during their free time away from school.

QUICKIE STRATEGY: BOOK COVERS

Decorate your walls with books checked out from the local library; ask bookstores for covers from sample copies of books and magazines; and encourage students to create collages of their favorite books.

3 Create an Awesome Classroom Library

The cornerstone of all my classrooms has been my classroom library. If you really want to get your students excited about reading, you need to make your classroom library more appealing than Disneyland.

Consider all the senses when you construct your classroom library. Make sure students have easy access to all reading materials. I learned the value early on of walking around my classroom on my knees and seeing my classroom from my young students' points of view. Create a visually appealing library that attracts lots of attention with its bright colors and awesome décor (e.g., I've created classroom libraries that looked like jungles or oceans, placed tents in some classroom libraries so students could read inside them with flashlights, and placed Christmas lights around others to dazzle my students). Spray some air freshener or brew some coffee near your classroom library so it smells good. Let students eat and drink while they read. Am I kidding? No. I like to eat and drink while I read, and, in my experience, students spill a lot less frequently than their parents at Back-to-School Night. Finally, play music in the classroom library.

Like every environmental trip I have provided so far, my goal is to create an experience that leaves my students hungry to read as much as possible.

4 Get Cool Things to Read

Access to reading materials is one of my passions, and I think it is great if you have 5000 books in your classroom library. But if you have 5000 copies of Norman Vincent Peale's *The Power of Positive Thinking*, I am willing to bet that your kids are not going to get turned on to reading.

Good teachers eavesdrop. If you hear your kids talking about NASCAR, get some books about NASCAR. If they are talking about Jennifer Lopez, place a biography of Jennifer Lopez in your classroom library. Remember: the school was built for the students, not the teachers. I learned long ago that while I have certain books that I want to expose my students to, not all of my book picks are going to turn kids on to reading.

Make sure to provide plenty of different types of reading materials, as well. Some kids don't like books. Besides showcasing a variety of different books, why not put a bunch of different magazines in your classroom library? When I was a kid, all I liked to do was eat. My teacher made sure to place plenty of menus before me to get me interested in reading.

Newspapers are a wonderful resource for teachers. I provide tons of newspapers to students, as newspapers are inexpensive, contain something of interest for just about everybody, and promote the daily reading habit I try to inspire in my students. Some can also be found for free in front of a lot of restaurants. The Newspapers in Education program even provides free newspapers and lesson plan packets to students and teachers. For more information on how to use newspapers in your classroom, check out my book, *News Flash! Newspaper Activities to Meet Language-Arts Standards & Differentiate Instruction.*

Comic books and football cards are wonderful ways to attract the attention of reluctant readers, especially boys. A lot of the best readers I know began with comic books.

Get some Leap Frog books in your classroom. I always feel like an old guy when I talk about Leap Frog because I wish the books had talked when I was a kid.

Provide multilingual books in your classroom, even if you have monolingual students. Students should hear different languages. I used to work at an inner-city preschool that served predominantly Spanish-speaking students, and one day we received a donation of books in Italian. Now, I don't read or write Italian, but I can decode it with an obnoxious pizzeria accent. My little preschoolers used to laugh during my Italian read-alouds, and now one of them has grown up to be an Italian major in college. You never know how you may affect a child.

Finally, provide plenty of reference books, as well. Every class I have ever taught has at least one boy who is a fountain of useless information. "Mr. Brassell, the state capital of Vermont is Montpelier!" "Great, Sergio," I'd say. "Can you go look up some more random facts from your almanac and tell me about them tomorrow?" And Sergio would dive back into his almanac to learn about Academy Award winners, population density, and obesity statistics in America.

The point is, different students have different reading interests, so we need to pay close attention to those interests and supply reading materials that will attract our students to reading.

QUICKIE STRATEGY: NO PUNISHMENT

Don't use reading as a punishment. I let my kids eat and drink, sit anywhere, and listen to music while they read. I made them run laps during physical education. Translation: I was a horrible physical fitness instructor, but my students loved reading time.

5 Find a Cool Place to Read

Comfort is king! Where do you like to read at home? In bed? On the sofa? On the toilet? Put these things in your classroom. Well, make sure you have a "no deposit" policy if you put a toilet in your classroom.

To get kids to love reading, we need to offer them plenty of comfortable places where they can read. I used to have teachers when I was a kid tell us all to sit at our seats and quietly read our books for 10 minutes. Our seats were not all that comfortable to begin with, and sitting like statues for 10 minutes was not a pleasurable experience for six-, seven-, and eight-year-old children.

If your students want to read under the table, let them. If they want to lie on the floor, let them. If they prefer to stand and lean against a wall, let them. We are trying to promote sensory experiences that allow students to relate reading to fun.

I used to provide plenty of cushions for students to sit on while they read. Another tip I have for teachers is to go to carpet stores and ask for free carpet samples for your

students. Sometimes I would get bed sheets and put them over tables so students could act like they were on camping trips reading. You can even create "reading pools" by filling old wading pools with newspapers and allowing students to read in there. A trip to the local thrift store usually provides a lot of inspiration for how to create inexpensive areas for relaxing reading.

6 Read While Students Read

When you ask students to read, that is not the time for you to eat your lunch or grade papers. Kids are not stupid. They know that if adults are not reading, they probably don't need to be reading. Teachers send signals with everything they do, and one of the areas I emphasize most to teachers is the importance of reading while students read.

Don't get me wrong. You do not have to read children's books while your students read. You can read whatever you want. As a matter of fact, I encourage teachers to read all of those books, newspapers, and magazines that they never seem to find time to read at home. Students need to see the pleasures of reading, and what better role model than to see a teacher who actively reads when students do?

My students were always curious about what I read, so I would always talk to them about what I was reading and what they were reading after we finished our reading time. (Teachers always ask me how much free reading time I permitted in my classroom. While I encourage at least 30 minutes a day for teachers of young children, I broke up my free-reading time into chunks of 7 to 10 minutes.) Inevitably, I had a couple of boys who refused to read anything on their own, so I would invite them to read the sports page with me or review a joke book or something else that got them to request the reading materials for their own personal use. If students see teachers excited about reading, the chances are high that they will be excited to be reading.

My colleagues and I started a book club at my school, where students saw us exchanging mysteries by Mary Higgins Clark or thrillers by Sydney Sheldon. You can also ask your school librarian to make a display of teachers' favorite books. I guarantee those books will draw high interest from students. It does not matter what you read; what matters most is that your students see you actively involved with reading. Simple modeling is still one of your best teaching techniques.

QUICKIE STRATEGY: AUTHOR READERS

Play books on tape read by the authors. I wanted my students to learn about the authors of their favorite books. When students learn about author backgrounds and where authors get their ideas, they become better readers and writers.

7 Word Wheels

My eyes used to wander all the time when I was a student, so to combat the daydreaming bug as a teacher, I decided to surround my students with as much print as possible. There was print on the floors, on the backs of chairs, and even on the ceiling (where I posted all the lyrics to our class songs).

I used to create word wheels to function as a center, serve as a model for a game students could create to take

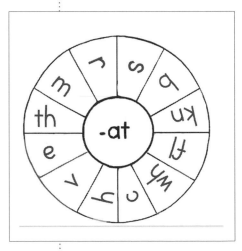

home, and provide a constant visual reminder of different phonograms that my students needed to become familiar with. Depending on which linguist you ask, there are between 37 and 39 phonograms that basically comprise over 500 of the most frequently used words in the written English language. It is essential to familiarize students with patterns in words, so I surrounded my students with various word wheels.

You can create a large word wheel to post on a bulletin board, allowing students to "spin the wheel" and create different words. For example, the "-at" word wheel would have the phonogram "-at" in the center, with letters and blends on the circumference. In a box to the left of "-at," students would sound out the word that was formed by combining the letter or blend with the phonogram (e.g., bat, cat, knat, flat, etc.).

At the word wheel center, my students would recreate smaller versions of the word wheels to take home and play with for practice. Rather than recreate a ton of different word wheels for every phonogram, the students learned to use sticky notes of phonograms to place in the centers of their word wheels. Word wheels are easy to make, cheap, and can be used to review a number of learning standards.

QUICKIE STRATEGY: NO DUMBING-DOWN

Don't "dumb down" your own reading. Just because you teach early elementary school students does not mean you have to read picture books in front of your students. Dive right into that Janet Evanovich or Dan Brown book you've wanted to read.

8 Color Codes

Fill your classroom with color, but use colors to distinguish things such as genres, curricular areas, and preferred readings. Especially for younger students, colors can be used as excellent classroom management tools.

For example, I used to work with a teacher who had three bookshelves labeled "easy books," "so-so books," and "tough books." The books on each shelf had a color to designate their difficulty ("easy" books had green labels, "so-so" books had yellow labels, and "tough" books had red labels). Her first graders kept on pulling books solely from the shelves labeled "tough books," even though many of her little ones were not yet reading at that level. Then one day she came up with the brilliant idea of re-labeling the bookshelves "tough books," "tougher books," and "toughest books," and all of her students began taking books from all three shelves, despite the fact that the color labels remained unchanged. What her expertise demonstrated to me was the power of teachers to set the tone for students.

I used to use colors in my classroom to create moods. My students labeled books blue when they were depressing and yellow when they were funny. I'd also use colors when facilitating jigsaws with students (for example, "blue" students would focus on characters, "red" students would focus on settings, "yellow" students would focus on plot, etc.), where various students' colors would designate their focus of expertise as they read (e.g., reviewing story elements, examining characters' points of view, etc.). I've also seen teachers use colors to demonstrate parts of speech, affixes, phonograms, etc. You can use colors to code the various genres of your classroom library, as I observed from an amazing teacher who had yellow shelves for fiction, blue shelves for nonfiction, green shelves for poetry, and red shelves for magazines. She also used different colors to divide genres into sub-genres.

9 Feelies and Knickknacks

Chances are you will have a lot of kinesthetic learners in your classroom. Most young children are touchy-feely, as evidenced by their wanting to hug you throughout the day. To make reading as remarkable an experience as possible, I tried to provide as many "feelies" as possible for my students.

Feelies can be a variety of objects. We used to have a "soothing basket" in my classroom filled with knickknacks like toy soldiers, racquetballs, hair scrunchies, cotton balls, and other inexpensive items from the discount store that some students would take to squeeze or hold as they read. Make sure to have centers with pipe cleaners, Legos, Wikki Stix, and paperclips for students to practice forming letters and words. I used to have centers with sand and salt to allow students to practice writing with their fingers, and I would also let students write with water on the chalkboard (a good way to clean it by the way). I also had a center with Silly Putty that students enjoyed using to capture print off newspapers.

A good way to get students interested in reading is letting them "feel" what they read. Have plenty of felt books in your classroom. Provide hook and loop bulletin boards where students can post felt letters. I liked to give students other knickknacks to use when they read, like sticky notes for finding the most important pieces of information in nonfiction stories and highlighting tape for textbooks. You may even want to help students create cubes for small group story starters and questions (e.g., the six sides of the cube could ask different questions about story elements or student reactions to reading).

QUICKIE STRATEGY: TEASE READING

Tease students constantly. Read aloud passages to students that leave them salivating for more. Guess which book your students will want to take home or read tomorrow in class?

10 Student-Created Labels/Realia

Here is a message to all those teachers out there who have all those beautiful and expensive teacher supply store items posted to their walls: take them all down. Let your children re-label everything in the classroom. It will be a messier classroom, but it will be their classroom. Remember what I said earlier—the school was built for the students, not the teachers. Students are more likely to pay attention to text that they create on their own.

For younger students, labels are a wonderful way to familiarize students with sight words. I liked to encourage students to create labels in multiple languages besides English, as well. I have noticed when you have labels that you stare at repeatedly, their messages tend to stick (that's why children are able to recognize labels on items at the grocery store). If you really want to get students paying attention to the world around them, ask them to create labels for their homes, as well. I have asked principals to allow my students to decorate the entire school with labels.

My students and I would also create "big books" or poster boards filled with labels for various situations and settings (e.g., at the doctor's office, grocery store, auto shop, etc.). Big books are larger versions of stories with large text that enable students to follow along as a teacher reads a story aloud. Wikipedia defines a big book as "an enlarged version of a beginning reading book, usually illustrated and with very large type, generally used by a group of students to read together and learn about concepts of print and various reading strategies." Kids simply define big books as fun.

You can also turn labeling into a game, where students are given a set of index cards with labels and they have to run around the room and place the labels on the correct items. Also, ask the class to label the parts of a book (e.g., cover, author, illustrator, spine, etc.).

QUICKIE STRATEGY: STUDENT RECOMMENDATIONS

Ask students for book recommendations. Amazingly, all humans love their opinions to be appreciated. Next, make sure you actually read what your students recommend.

11 Book Baskets

One of my biggest pet peeves when I was teaching young children occurred whenever students finished a project early and shouted, "I'm done!" I always felt like I was a chef and would ask my students, "Are you medium rare?" A simple way for me to avoid this headache was to place book baskets on my students' tables.

I typically organized my students into groups of four and placed the book baskets at the centers of the tables. I instructed students to pick out a book whenever they completed an activity. In this way I could keep tabs on who was finishing early and when I needed to move on to something else. Also, I recently noticed that children's books are a lot shorter than adult-level books, so one of your jobs as your students' teacher is to ensure that books are rotated routinely so Pablo is not always stuck reading the same book every single day (unless that is what he wants to do, which is perfectly fine by me).

I was a bit of a neat freak with my students, and I found that an added bonus of having book baskets on each group's table was that I could facilitate a friendly competition among tables to see who kept their book baskets tidiest. If you cannot remember to rotate the book baskets every week or so, then assign that responsibility to student helpers. Book baskets can also be used for "musical chairs reading" and reviews of different genres (e.g., you could load one book basket with just historical fiction, another with poetry, etc., and make a game where students have to guess their book basket's genre). I even held contests for my students to see which group could decorate their book baskets the most creatively, using different fairy tales, nursery rhymes, or other literary genres as themes.

12 Rain-Gutter Bookshelves

My friend and mentor, Jim Trelease, gave me this idea, and it is one of the most popular and practical ideas that I present at workshops. Go to a hardware store like Lowe's or The Home Depot and purchase rain gutters. They are fairly inexpensive, and for a little bit more you can purchase the hangers that hold them up. Most janitors will help you install the rain gutters on your classroom walls. Why do this? Well, now you have bookshelves that allow the book covers to face forward. Marketing is just as important in reading as it is in any other venture.

In my studies of students' reading habits over the last 15 years, I have found that students tend to select two types of books: books that have been read aloud by teachers and books with cool covers. Rain-gutter bookshelves market covers the way most grocery stores market boxes of cereal. Have you ever approached grocery store managers and suggested they could fit a lot more boxes of cereal on their shelves if they put the boxes in sideways? Of course not; grocery stores know that children are more likely to want an item when they see a cool picture of a silly bunny or an Olympic athlete.

I convinced a friend to use rain-gutter bookshelves, and she said it was the single-greatest decision she ever made. She hated creating bulletin boards for her classroom. The rain-gutter bookshelves not only provided tons of books to entice students and added lots of color to her classroom, they also blocked any space that could be used for bulletin boards. The moral: publicizing books with rain-gutter bookshelves can ultimately save a teacher a lot of work!

13 Computers and the Internet

I have found a lot of students who are reluctant to read Jane Austen but can surf the Internet for hours on end. I was working with a fourth grader whose teacher told me he did not like to read. She also told me Victor was "illiterate." I worked with him for one hour, and in the first 25 minutes Victor had at least 12 different windows opened on the Internet; he had text-messaged a couple of friends and sent e-mail messages to a few others. Victor was not illiterate by any means; he was highly literate in a 21st century sense. His biggest obstacle was a teacher who did not understand the computer Victor treasured.

There is really no excuse any longer for teachers not to encourage students to use computers frequently. While many schools do not have the resources to purchase a lot of the latest educational software, there are plenty of free resources available on the Internet.

One of my favorite Internet tools is YouTube.com, which hosts millions of videos, including a growing database of sample teacher lessons (www.teachertube.com is also a wonderful resource for teachers interested specifically in watching sample lessons, different classrooms, etc.). One video that intrigued me in particular (http://youtube.com/watch?v=GES3um1HYcm) reveals a lot of interesting tidbits in under six minutes, including:

- The number of text messages sent each day exceeds the population of the planet.

- According to former Secretary of Education Richard Riley, the top 10 jobs that will be in demand in 2010 did not exist in 2004.

- The U.S. is 20th in the world in broadband Internet penetration (Luxembourg recently passed us).

- One of every eight couples married in 2007 met online.

- There are over 106 million registered users of MySpace (as of Sept. 2006). If MySpace were a country, it would be the 11th largest in the world (between Japan and Mexico).

In training thousands of teachers across the country, I have learned that most teachers have no idea of the number of free, useful Web sites available to them. The Internet is a wonderful tool to enhance teachers' teaching by using it for:

- Virtual library search engine

- Graphics

- Utility programs (e.g., grade books)

- Professional information (e.g., credential regulations, standards, grants, jobs, etc.)

- Document retrieval (e.g., public domain books, poetry, song lyrics, etc.)

- Virtual field trips

  * www.artsedge.kennedy-center.org (The Kennedy Center)
  * www.metmuseum.org/(The Metropolitan Museum of Art)
  * www.playmusic.org (teaches students instruments in the orchestra)

- Lesson plans

- Simulations and games

Check out the extensive list of free Web resources at the back of the book.

14 Word Walls with Words

I am a big advocate for teaching vocabulary words in a number of ways. Why? We know that 300 words make up 65% of all written material contained in newspaper articles, magazines, textbooks, children's stories, and novels. Helping students become familiar with these first 300 words is a great way to build their reading confidence. One of the most popular ways teachers expose students to these "high-frequency words" is the word wall. Here is my advice for teachers constructing word walls: put words on them!

I have observed thousands of elementary school classrooms, and almost every classroom has a word wall. And almost every one of those word walls is missing one thing: words. If you're not going to use it, put up some rain-gutter bookshelves to make the wall more useful to students.

What are the first words that should go up on that word wall? Students' names need to be up there, and I'd probably start the year with the top 25 high-frequency words. I usually recommend adding five to seven new words each week. You do not want to overwhelm the students. I have witnessed some classrooms where the teacher posted 800 words to start the year, and little Sephra and Kyara were fearing the coming months. I usually also added keywords from our readings, along with words students had brought from home. Listing words in their vernacular on a word wall can aid students' understanding of academic vocabulary.

The point is that word walls are only useful if teachers use them in assisting students with words they encounter frequently. Make your word wall fun and memorable, and spend just a little bit of time each day showing students how to use the word wall as a reference tool.

15 Dioramas from Shoe Boxes

Comprehension activities do not have to drain students' interest in reading. I see so many teachers who assign book reports all the time as the sole measure of a student's reading comprehension, and it drives me crazy. Please remember these three words: book reports stink. They drive students from reading. There are all sorts of ways to determine what students take away from the stories they read. Dioramas remain popular with my students.

Take out a shoe box and recreate scenes from what you read. That's about it. Early elementary school students are interested in art, and many students

enjoy working with their hands. I have had boys who had no interest whatsoever in explaining to me what they read, but once I handed them a shoe box and art supplies, they suddenly could re-create beautiful scenes from their books.

Not only are dioramas wonderful showcases of what students have read, they also brighten up classrooms and provide constant advertisements to students and their parents about the wonders that can be found in books. For teachers who hate bulletin boards, dioramas can be stapled onto a bulletin board along with brief narratives to retell different stories and teach students about story elements, sequence of events, and a number of other standards. In this way, I turned my classroom into a "museum," filled with students' dioramas of different stories we'd read covering a variety of subject areas. Most importantly, though, dioramas offer teachers a fun, alternative way to differentiate instruction for students.

QUICKIE STRATEGY: FUN OPTION

Whenever your class faces a dreary task (e.g., cleaning desks or anything else you have identified that your students do not like), give them the option of that task or reading. Reading will always come out the winner, and students tend to develop an attitude that reading is the "fun" option.

CHAPTER 2

Talk

Talk is not cheap. Talk is very valuable. The more language students are exposed to, the better. In my mind, the louder the classroom, the more learning is taking place. If students are not talking about books, *you* need to be talking about books.

When I worked at a radio station as a disc jockey (yes, I have had plenty of different jobs in my lifetime), my boss used to emphasize that the most cardinal sin to commit was to allow "dead air." Dead air is the gap between songs or pauses in talking. When a person flips through radio stations and comes across dead air, that person is likely to change the channel. I do not want dead air in my classroom. While my students were surrounded by plenty of print in the classroom, they were also surrounded by plenty of conversations, speeches, and performances.

Not all students are talkers, and that is fine. If students are not talking, however, they need to hear lots of models talking. I constantly asked my students about what they read and what they liked to read, but I also shared with students books and articles that I enjoyed. I did whatever I could to excite my students about reading, even acting like different characters from stories (I lost my personal pride long ago, during my first year of teaching).

I was never a quiet kid, so I empathize with students who get in trouble for talking. When I see quiet students I usually wonder if they are timid, scared, or bored. At least when students are talking, I know they are engaged. One of my great teachers taught me years ago that the best way to get a student interested in reading is to find out what that student is interested in. If students are not talking, I can never find out what they like. Do whatever it takes to engage students in talking to you and with each other about books.

1 Read Aloud

When actor Yul Brynner passed away from lung cancer, he pre-taped a commercial for the American Lung Association in which he said, "Don't smoke. Whatever you do, don't smoke." Here's what I have to say to teachers: "Read aloud. Whatever you do, read aloud." One of the only things that almost everyone agrees on in education is that the students who are read aloud to do a lot better in reading.

Reading aloud is perhaps the most intimate way teachers can advertise the joys of reading to students. It also provides an excellent opportunity for students and teachers to discuss their thoughts and feelings as they read various texts. I believe that if teachers were allowed to spend at least 30 minutes each day reading aloud, then those students would read better than ones who were not exposed to read-alouds. I'd stake my entire professional career on that belief.

It doesn't matter how you read aloud, either. Everyone has her own style. I like to impersonate lots of different character voices, but I have seen less hyperactive teachers calmly recite the words from a special rocking chair. To me, the key to any successful read-aloud is making the experience memorable in some way.

Once students build up their confidence in reading, allow them to read aloud to you and the rest of the class. I know that I am not telling you anything new here, but I want to reaffirm to you that reading aloud is a very good idea, and it absolutely needs to be a part of your daily curriculum. One more suggestion: read poetry aloud. I read aloud at least four poems a day to my students, ranging from Jack Prelutsky and Shel Silverstein to Emily Dickinson and William Shakespeare. By the end of each year my students had been exposed to over 700 poems. Do you think their teachers the following year were grateful?

One more note: the single-greatest resource any teacher can own (besides my books) is Jim Trelease's *The Read-Aloud Handbook* (Penguin, 2006). Believe me, Jim does not need my help promoting his book, as it is in its sixth edition and remains one of the most popular education books of all time. You will find a treasure trove of research on the importance of reading aloud plus summaries of great books to read aloud to K–12 students.

QUICKIE STRATEGY: BOOK BAG RECOMMENDATIONS

Divide the class into small groups and create a book bag for each one. Set a short period of time for each student to scan one of his group's books and judge whether it is a book he would recommend (you can do variations of this, like "too hard, too easy, just right" or "thumbs up, thumbs down"). Students write their recommendations on a piece of paper, and, after the timer goes off, pass their books clockwise to the person beside them in the group. After all the books have made their way into the hands of all small-group members, ask students to discuss.

2 Book Talks

I used to have a teacher who always began class by telling us what he was reading, and then he allowed us to share what we were reading. What ever happened to book talks? One of the best ways to promote books is to talk about great books. I know one of the easiest ways to get me to read anything is to hear a friend recommend a particular book.

Whenever I conducted book talks with my students (which was at least once a week), I shared a variety of genres and levels, as I wanted to provide the greatest variety possible. Consider the interests of your students, and plan accordingly. I recommend John Grisham books to kindergartners. Why? I want students to see that reading becomes a lifelong addiction, and there are fabulous materials out there to meet all interests.

How do you get a student interested in a book? I spoke at a conference of 800 first-grade teachers and realized I was one of the only men in the room. When I asked teachers to tell me their favorite books to read to students, I noticed that just about every book named had a furry animal in it. While I like furry animals, I can assure you that many boys (who represent the majority of reluctant readers, by the way) only like books about furry animals if something bad happens to those furry animals. Again, it is always important to know and understand your audience. My mother used to talk to my brother and me all the time about football stories she read in the newspaper. It was not until I was an adult that I discovered that she hates football, but she made sure to read about it so she would be able to talk to my brother and me. That's the kind of dedication great teachers reveal, as I found my library of *Captain Underpants* and *The Magic Treehouse* grow over the years.

One more tip: whenever you give a book talk, include some cliffhangers. I loved to introduce students to *Salt in His*

Shoes by Deloris Jordan. The book chronicles the real-life childhood of basketball superstar Michael Jordan. He misses a shot that loses a game for his team, and asks his mother how he can get better. She tells him to practice harder every day and put salt in his shoes every night so he'll grow. He does both religiously every day and takes the final shot in a game a year later. When students asked if he made it, I'd tell them to read the book for themselves.

QUICKIE STRATEGY: FAVORITE PASSAGES

Allow students to share with the class parts of books and poems they enjoy. Ask students to explain what about their passage they like.

3 Book Discussions

To me, a book discussion is a little different from a book talk. I am not a fan of educational jargon, so you may call these different activities whatever you like. It is only important to understand the difference. I believe book talks are opportunities for teachers and students to discuss their favorite books. A book discussion, in my opinion, is when everybody has read the same book and discusses their reactions to it.

I believe good readers are picky readers. I will do something now for you: for all of you who have a large book on your bedside table that you started reading three years ago, I absolve you of that book. Get another one. The reason Americans don't read a lot, I suspect, is the same reason we are mostly overweight: we're taught to finish what we start. Well, that's not always wise. Think of a book like a piece of food. If you take a bite and find it repulsive, do you take another bite? So why keep reading if the first chapter does not hold your attention? Put that book down, and get another.

Book discussions provide wonderful opportunities for students to share and defend their reactions to what they read. I often audiotaped or videotaped book discussions, and sometimes I even sent them to authors. I wanted students to develop an understanding of their own reading tastes, as well as an appreciation for the qualities of good books. Lively book discussions tend to inspire students to look for deeper understandings of what they read, and many students simply get a kick out of dismissing a book or insisting it is the best thing they have ever discovered.

QUICKIE STRATEGY: READING TIMELINES

Reading timelines are a fun way to allow students to share their favorite books through different periods in their lives. "My favorite book way back in kindergarten was *Where the Wild Things Are*," one of my first graders once said. "But this year I've become a bigger fan of *Junie B. Jones*."

4 Role Play/Put It in Your Own Words

One of the ways to encourage students to read is to put stories into their own words and contexts. For example, if we were reading *Little Red Riding Hood*, students could change the forest to their neighborhood, make the wolf a hungry stranger, and switch the goodies in Little Red Riding Hood's basket. Your students are more likely to relate to a story if you put it into a context they understand.

For example, I changed names in stories all the time in order to capture students' attention. I have read a lot of books that feature a Bobby or Dick or Jane, but I have never taught a Bobby or Dick or Jane. So my stories were about Juanito and Amir and Tanisha because I taught students by those names. Children are more likely to get involved with a story when they hear names they are familiar with. When I was a child, one of my favorite books was called *Danny and the Dinosaur*. It did not take a rocket scientist to figure out why.

One way to encourage role plays is to read aloud a story to your class, then ask students to team up with a partner to create their own version of a story. The only rule is that they have to change some or all elements of the story (beware of telling students they can change all elements of a story. I once had a little boy change every element of a story, to the point of his version being completely different in every way from the original). After students create their own versions of stories, you can ask them to perform it live, record it, create a book about it, draw pictures of their version—the possibilities for differentiation are limitless.

5 Ghost Stories with Flashlights

Like it or not, you need to constantly keep your students entertained. Students get bored easily, so you need to keep reading a fresh and fun experience. One of my favorite things to do with students was to read aloud ghost stories. Keep in mind when you read ghost stories that younger students enjoy the kind of ghost stories that end in "Boo!" Some of the ghost stories I see teachers read are a little too scary for young children, and I do not want to be responsible for children's nightmares.

Whenever I read aloud ghost stories with students, I liked to turn off the class lights and place a flashlight under my chin (under my chin signaled ghost stories, profiling my face signaled a romance). Some students with behavior problems, in my experience, will actually cease negative behavior when promised a ghost story.

The students and I liked to write ghost stories and read them aloud to parents and other classes. Here is one fun story the kids and I created together (make sure to divide students into two teams, with one team reading the text on the left and the other reading the text on the right):

• The night was	Dark, dark, dark.
• I walked up to a	Dark, dark, dark house.
• And knocked on the	Dark, dark, dark door.
• "Hallo," I said.	Nobody answered.
• So I walked through the	Dark, dark, dark door.
• I walked through the	Dark, dark, dark hallway.
• And I entered a	Dark, dark, dark room.
• "Hallo," I said.	Nobody answered.
• I walked over to a	Dark, dark, dark chest.
• I opened it, and out came a	Dark, dark, dark GHOST!

Whenever we read as a class, we "choral read." I was in a choir when I was a kid, and I'd sing "Amazing Grace" at the top of my lungs and mouth the rest of the words. It didn't matter that I did not know the rest of the song because 30 other kids had my back. And after a few weeks, I figured out the rest of the words. I never forgot the kindness of my teacher who never put me on the spot until she knew I could succeed. Since I had a lot of shy students and ESL students, I practiced a "strength in numbers" philosophy that encouraged students to read aloud together. The point is to make the reading aloud of any ghost story a fun experience that students always associate positively in their minds with reading.

QUICKIE STRATEGY: STUDENT REPORTER

Ask students to find a partner. One student acts like a reporter, and the other student acts like a character or author or other "VIBP (Very Important Book Person)." The reporter asks questions to learn more about an author's or character's motivation (in this way, both students have the opportunity to reflect on what they read).

6 Australian Pete

People need variety. In his book *Purple Cow*, Seth Godin chronicles the importance of getting people's attention. He suggests that if you travel along the countryside for the first time and have never seen a cow, you are amazed the first time you see one. You continue to point out the cow on subsequent trips, but each time it becomes a little less noticeable. After a while, you hardly notice the cow. Then, one day, you see a purple cow, and the cycle begins again. The same cycle is played out in classrooms across America on a daily basis.

My students might have enjoyed an activity the first few times I tried it, but after a while it grew into a stale routine. One of the ways I tried to make my read-alouds come to life was by inviting special "guest readers." For example, when I noticed my students getting antsy, I'd tell them that I had invited "Australian Pete" to come read to the class. I'd leave the classroom for a brief moment, strut back in like I had just returned from the Outback, and with a tip of my imaginary bush hat, say, "G'day, mates. I just got done puttin' a shrimp on the barbie. Your teacher says you want me to read to you?" My students would jump up in cheers, shouting, "Yeah, it's Australian Pete!" Keep in mind it was me, with a silly accent.

I'd do the same thing at the end of the day when the students were acting restless and driving me crazy. "All right, kids, if you don't want me, I guess I have to get Grumpy Old Man to come read to you." Then I'd briefly exit and return with a slouch and scowl saying, "Shut up, you little twerps. Your teacher told me to read to you!" My students would applaud and eat it up, but I will warn you that Grumpy Old Man backfired on me once when a parent came to my class and asked, "Did some mean elderly man tell the kids to be quiet?" I just nodded and said I'd make sure never to invite the "Grumpy Old Man" back to my classroom.

Whatever it takes to make reading a memorable activity, do it. My students might have forgotten a lot of my scripted reading exercises, but they never forgot a guest reader.

QUICKIE STRATEGY: CHIPS IN THE POT

Buy poker chips (or clothespins or some other small token) at the store, and write student names on the individual chips. Distribute them to the students. Start a discussion that will involve the entire class, and tell students they may only comment when they place their chip in the "pot." You can also give each student more than one chip because some students may want to follow up on an idea without having to wait for the entire class to drop in their chips and speak.

7 Compare and Contrast/Point of View

I used to have a little girl in class named Elizabeth who always sat in a way that suggested she was going to die from boredom. One day, my principal at the time walked into my classroom to do her daily evaluation of my teaching, and she chose to ask Elizabeth what she was doing. Looking as bored as always and not moving a muscle, Elizabeth lamented, "Mr. Brassell has us doing Venn diagrams comparing and contrasting Bob Cratchett and Ebeneezer Scrooge from Charles Dickens's *A Christmas Carol*, and he says if we do a good job we get to listen to *The Nutcracker Suite* by Tchaikovsky." I guess she was listening after all!

Pointing out similarities and differences between texts and encouraging students to make connections with what they read and their own lives, and with the world and other texts, is a great way to build students' reading comprehension. Additionally, it allows students to connect on a personal level with what they read. Finally, maybe it is the historian in me, but I love to get students thinking about the same event from different points of view.

QUICKIE STRATEGY: WHAT'S NEWS?

I love newspapers, so I encourage students to talk about different stories they come across during a time we call "What's News?"

8 Show and Tell

Bring back "Show and Tell." I repeat: bring back "Show and Tell." You may have to re-name it "Standards-based Sharing Time," but bring back "Show and Tell." Why? Human beings are naturally nosy. That's why most reading journals have subscription rates in the thousands and many tabloids boast circulation in the millions.

One of your priorities as a teacher is to encourage your students to work together. In order to do that, students need to bond with one another, and I find "Show and Tell" is essential for creating team spirit in a classroom. My students want to know about one another, and I want to know about them, too.

I have trained a lot of teachers who complained that in the present "test-craze" environment, "Show and Tell" may not be the best use of their time, and I would beg to differ. To me it's never a waste of time to find out about one's peers, and "Show and Tell" provides a forum for students to get to talk about themselves without fear of giving right or wrong answers. This is also an excellent opportunity to learn about student interests so you can figure out what materials they may be interested in reading. Ask them to present favorite reading materials while doing their "Show and Tell."

9 Morning Meeting/ Announcements

Why morning meeting? Students like being the teacher. If it were up to me, the entire day would be a morning meeting because kids remember so much more information when they teach it to one another. It takes about a month to train students how to run the morning meeting, and this is how the power shifts:

- Model—Teacher does.

- Guided Practice—Teacher/students do.

- Independent Practice—Students do.

During the first month of school, try to train your students how to run the morning meeting for themselves. Again, the more the teacher participates as an observer while the students lead the meeting, the better students learn.

Morning meetings provide numerous print encounters for students. As they prepare for their respective parts, students will read weather reports, newspaper articles, and relevant facts from the almanac.

In my classroom, morning meetings followed a routine format. After beginning the day with a song or chant (when Disney's *The Lion King* was popular, we began to call our singing circle the "circle of life," named after the hit Elton John song from the film), we used to run our morning meetings like news broadcasts:

- "Circle of Life" (songs: see Chapter 5, Strategy 13 for examples)

- Daily News

- Weather

- Famous Birthdays

- Thought of the Day
- Personal Profile
- Today's Agenda
- Class Goals & Objectives

When students arrived in my classroom, they could view their morning meeting roles posted on the wall. Note that the famous birthdays usually require a bit of practice and function as an excellent fluency exercise in Readers' Theatre (where students read aloud scripts of readings). Make sure to allow students at least a week to practice reciting the famous birthdays. Morning meeting roles look something like this:

- It's *Morning Meeting*, starring…
- Rogelio acting as the teacher
- Julietta serving as our anchorperson
- Juanito presenting the weather and plants report
- Lashonda reading us today's famous birthdays and fun facts
- Muriel sharing today's thought of the day
- Victor giving his personal profile
- Cynthia reviewing today's agenda
- And all of Room 12 reciting our goals and objectives for today!

Note that the teacher (in this case, Rogelio) is in charge of beginning the morning meeting and keeping everyone on task. This student is assigned at the end of school the previous day, and, after school, the classroom teacher reviews what that student will be doing the next day. Here are some typical scripts for each role:

Daily News

- Today is (day of the week).
- Today's date is (month, date, year).

- We have been in school for (#) days.

- There are (#) days left of school this year.

- The letter of the day is (letter).

- The number of the day is (#).

- The word of the day is (high-frequency word).

Weather

- The season is (season).

- Today it will be (weather adjective).

- The temperature outside is (#) degrees Fahrenheit.

- It is going to be a (descriptive adjective) day.

Famous Birthdays

- Today is the birthday of former President Grover Cleveland, race-car driver Mario Andretti, cellist Yo-Yo Ma, and Victor's baby sister.

- Today is cartoonist Stan Lee's birthday.

- Stan Lee is (#) years old.

- He lives in Brooklyn, New York.

- When he was little, he liked to draw pictures.

- He is famous because he created many comic strips.

- Stan Lee created *Spider Man.*

Thought of the Day

Two roads diverged in a wood
And I took the one less traveled by
And that has made all the difference.
–Robert Frost

Personal Profile

- Translation: Show and Tell!

Today's Agenda

- Math: We will practice counting by 2s, 5s, and 10s.

- Science: We will review the water cycle.

- Social Studies: We will perform our Black History Month play.

- Language Arts: We will write to our pen pals.

- When we complete these tasks (our goals for today), we will earn a reading party (a reading party was usually a "Fluffy Friday," when students would bring pillows to the classroom, and I would read stories to them as they lay on the floor).

Student Goals

- By the end of school today, I will… (encourage students to set individual goals, comparing their progress to themselves rather than one another).

Keep in mind that morning meetings may take anywhere from 10 to 45 minutes, but I assure you, when run properly, morning meetings facilitate meaningful, deeper learning among students.

QUICKIE STRATEGY: CLASS-READING RAP

Create a class-reading rap. Divide students into teams of four and give each team a phonogram (e.g., -at, -an, etc.). Each team must create a line for each of its members that relates to reading and uses the phonogram. For example, if Lilia, Santo, Jermaine, and Li were to get the phonogram "-at," they might come up with something like this: "Lilia loves reading cuz she's a cool cat, but Santo doesn't think books are all that. Jermaine reads faster than a flying bat, and Li loves to read on a comfy mat."

10 Read to a Stuffed Animal or Puppet

I once taught a little girl named Isabel whose family had just emigrated from Guatemala. Isabel did not speak a word of English. At least, I do not think she did, as she did not say a word in my class for the first two weeks of school. Determined to hear her speak, I brought a teddy bear to Isabel one day and said in Spanish, "Isabel, this teddy bear does not know how to read. Can you please teach him how?" Ten minutes later, I heard Isabel's voice for the first time. Granted, the book I gave Isabel was written in

English, and she was reading it aloud in Spanish. Baby steps, I always say. I was delighted to hear Isabel read aloud softly, "Habia una vez." Then, pointing the teddy bear's stuffed paw on the words, Isabel read in a perfect teddy bear-voice, "Habia una vez" (translated as "Once upon a time").

Remember: kids like being teachers. Let them.

I used to have lots of puppets for my students to play with, and two maintained homes on my desk. They were my English-speaking dragon, "Danny the Dragon," and my Spanish-speaking clown, "Pablo Payaso." I would let the two puppets conduct read-alouds, lead book talks, and discuss story elements with my students. The great thing about puppets, I found, was that students acted as if I were not around and spoke directly to the puppets on my hands. Many of my kinesthetic learners also enjoyed putting puppets on their hands to read along in stories.

You can get all sorts of cheap puppets and stuffed animals at garage sales and thrift stores. If you need to, you can always create puppets out of socks and other materials. I often used stuffed animals and puppets as an incentive, as

I would assure students that if they finished their work early I'd allow them to read with their puppets and stuffed animals. If you have not already tried them, you would be amazed at how popular stuffed animals and puppets can be with your students.

QUICKIE STRATEGY: COMMERCIALS

Ask students to create their own commercials advertising favorite books. They may act out their commercial in front of the class, audio-tape it, videotape it, re-enact it with puppets, etc. I've personally used audiotapes with kindergartners. I suspect that with a basic lesson, even first graders could use the video camera and a Mac.

11 Jokes and Riddles

I am going to give you a warning here and now: beware of telling young children jokes and riddles because once you start telling your students jokes and riddles, I have found that they will start telling you jokes and riddles. And I have had some little boys tell me the same riddle every single day. Every day their riddle had a new punch line, and every day that punch line was not funny.

I began telling my students jokes and riddles as a way to ensure they would come back promptly after recess and lunch breaks. However, I quickly learned that jokes and riddles were a tremendously enticing tool to get some students reading. Students who refused to read a paragraph in their textbooks could literally spend an afternoon reading hundreds of jokes in the pages of some silly book.

One of the games I used to play with my students was to create word riddles (puns) with them. We'd brainstorm vocabulary related to a concept like space, and we'd choose a word like "star" to focus on. We would drop off the initial letter and come up with as many words as we could think of that began with the remaining letters (e.g., Tarzan, target, tartar sauce, tardy). We would then put the initial letter back on the word and come up with word riddles, like, "What do you call spiders in outer space? Starantulas!" Trust me, second graders roll over laughing when they create such masterpieces.

12 The People's Court

I have found students are just like everyone else. What they really want is the right to gripe. So I created a center with a "case docket" book, and whenever student's had a problem, based on their level of literacy, they'd write their problem down, draw it, scribble it—whatever. Once we accomplished our goals for the day (I never taught "objectives," as typical human beings don't talk like that; they set goals), my students had "free choice time." One of the options available to them was called "The People's Court," modeled after the popular TV series *The People's Court*.

If students chose The People's Court (and it was one of the most popular activities in our class), I'd ask my "student of the day" to act as the bailiff and call court to order.

"All rise and raise your right hand," the bailiff would say. "Do you all swear to tell the truth, the whole truth, and nothing but the truth? If so, say 'I do.'"

After all the students repeated "I do," the bailiff asked them all to be seated.

"People's Court is now in session. The Honorable Judge Brassell presiding."

"Thank you, Madame Bailiff," I'd say. "Can you please read the first case?"

"Case #1," the bailiff read. "Omunique vs. José."

Now things would start swinging. It looked like a scene straight out of *Law and Order*. Students announced Omunique was the plaintiff and José was the defendant, and all of a sudden students were raising hands and begging to cross-examine the witnesses. What I learned above all else from this activity was that if I am ever on trial, I want none of my students on my jury. That's because my kids only knew one word: guilty.

"This court hereby finds the defendant, José, guilty of hitting Omunique," I announced. "But, as honesty is the best policy, and José confessed to his offense, I hereby sentence José to apologize to Omunique and give her a hug."

All the kids would cheer, and half the time the students had made up the argument in the first place so they would have the chance to play The People's Court. Like any good activity, The People's Court is fun, engaging, and covers at least 10 various standards in the curricula (it's worth doing just for the oral language practice alone).

13 Books on Tape/ Listening Centers

One of God's gifts to teachers is the local discount store, which offers endless possibilities for imaginative teachers and their students. I can get 10 old cassettes at a discount store for under a dollar, and then record books on tape for my students to listen to in their listening centers (a lot of stores sell tape recorders for around $5, and I get earphones donated from friends). Students are more likely to listen to a book on tape when it is read aloud by a familiar, significant figure: a teacher, parent, older sibling, or friend, preferably.

Whenever I recorded books on tape, I made the sound "ding-dong" whenever I wanted the student to turn a page. Once students advanced to a level where they were creating their own books on tape, they would say "ding-dong" when they wanted readers to turn the page. This is my "pyramid scheme." Some day I want the entire world saying "ding-dong" whenever they turn a page.

I love recording books on tape, and I would encourage students to record books on tape for a number of reasons. First, many parents will claim they do not know how to read, so you simply send the tapes home so the parents can play the tapes. The tapes are also great for automobiles (yes, if you have more advanced technology, I encourage you to use podcasts, burn CDs, etc.). Also, I have had a lot of students who like to perform, and books on tape permit them to shine in such a format. Finally, I loved getting my students to create books on tape and donate them to other classes or younger grades (or hospitals and senior centers) because my students beamed with pride whenever they created a product to serve a thankful audience.

QUICKIE STRATEGY: FAMOUS QUOTATIONS

Hand students various quotes from famous people and have them read aloud their quote normally; then have them impersonate the famous person delivering the quote. You can listen to a number of famous speeches on www.americanrhetoric. com. This game is especially fun when students act like various Presidents of the United States.

14 Partner Read

Do you have some students who just cannot stop talking? You can either allow them to create a disturbance, or you can allow them to talk. My mother has never received a piece of mail that she did not feel compelled to read aloud to every single person in the room. I love to tell people about interesting sports stories I come across in the newspaper. Some of my students just loved pointing out cool pictures or amazing facts they came across when reading, and I believe as teachers we need to encourage this. Rather than having students constantly interrupt my personal reading, I matched my "talkers" as partners and allowed them to read together.

Partners do not have to read the same text, mind you. All that matters is that they have someone else that they can share their thoughts with because some students just feel like talking about what they read as they read. There is nothing wrong with this, and I encouraged it in a way that did not disrupt other readers. By recognizing beforehand that some students loved to talk as they read, I could proactively manage my class. I'd give all of my students partners, carefully matching my silent readers in pairs and my talkers in pairs. Talkers read anywhere, but they had to keep their voices at a level where the rest of the class could still hear the music we were listening to. After our reading time, I solicited feedback from all students about what they were reading, thus allowing my talkers to share with the whole class what they had been reading.

Again, there is nothing earth-shattering or revelatory in letting students read in pairs. I simply believe that this is an overlooked strategy that can help promote positive reading experiences in students.

15 Book Buddies / Reading Volunteers

It does not take a rocket scientist to figure out why Marie Clay's Reading Recovery program works so well. Reading Recovery is a short-term intervention of one-to-one tutoring for low-achieving first graders in which individual students receive a half-hour lesson each school day for 12 to 20 weeks with a specially trained Reading Recovery teacher. As soon as students can meet grade-level expectations and demonstrate they can continue to work independently in the classroom, their lessons are discontinued, and new students begin individual instruction.

This is the same premise behind the work I do training parents, volunteers, and older siblings and peers to work with struggling and reluctant readers. Give me a book buddy or reading volunteer working one-on-one with a child for an hour a week over a six-month period, and I assure you that that child is going to become a better and happier reader. Parents, community members, older siblings, and students in upper grades all make great book buddies and reading volunteers.

I train volunteers and book buddies to structure their hour into six 10-minute blocks, as the average American has an attention span of about 10 minutes. The six "blocks" consist of talking with the child, promoting books through a book talk, selecting a book to perform a "picture read," reading aloud a story to the child, reading aloud a book in sync with the child, and, finally, playing games and writing with a child. Often, volunteers find that they cannot complete all six blocks within an hour, so some activities are pushed to the following week. The two activities that I emphasize need to be done each session with the child are to read aloud *to* the child (which, in my opinion, is the best way to improve any person's reading) and to read aloud *with* the child.

If you cannot attract parent or community volunteers, talk to an upper-grade-level teacher and ask for his discipline problems. Some of the best teachers, I have found, are often misunderstood students. Giving those students the responsibility of working with a younger child tends to decrease any discipline problems they may have and increase their daily attendance. In my experience, while struggling and reluctant readers benefit immensely from this program, reading volunteers and book buddies enjoy the opportunity to work with their students and often ask to work with more.

CHAPTER 3

Class Systems

Probably one of the most controversial things I used to do as a teacher was refuse to teach language arts. That's right: I never taught language arts, or math or science or social studies. Rather, my students and I learned about language arts, math, social studies, and science throughout the day. We did not have "math time" because I thought that was a disservice to students. Life is about lots of things happening at once, and I do not see how block scheduling adequately prepares students for life.

Instead, I used systems or procedures in my classroom that encouraged students to use language arts, math, social studies, and science throughout the day. One must be able to read no matter what the subject area, so we can practice fluency just as easily while practicing a concept in math as we could during a specified time of the day called "fluency practice." I wanted my students to see how they could apply skills to different situations. Reading is essential to just about everything students need to learn and understand, so it should be easily and naturally integrated into systems throughout the day.

One final note about class systems: I always had a policy in my class that if we created a routine, my job was to train my students how to run the routine. The more students run your class, the better. Students learn more by doing, and I encourage teachers to hand over the reins of power and allow students to teach themselves as much as possible.

1 Line Reading

I travel through a lot of airports, and inevitably I get stuck behind a gentleman in the TSA security line who taps his foot, checks his watch, and openly gripes aloud to no one in particular about how long the TSA officers take. I am always stuck behind this person, and I have to grin because it does not bother me at all. I have learned to always keep a book on hand as my constant travel companion.

One of the true pleasures I wish to impart to students is to always have something to read. Petty annoyances turn into moments I look forward to, as long as I have something to read. The world would be a much more peaceful place, I am convinced, if everyone had something to read. Reading good books relaxes people, and I know I am having an impact on my students if the recess bell rings and they do not rush out the doors immediately because they want to finish a chapter.

Line reading is easy to practice with students, and my students always went to lunch with something to read in hand. They could have a book or newspaper or magazine or poem—what they had did not matter to me. One of the benefits of a school where the average cafeteria wait was 15–20 minutes was training my students to bring something to read. Did some books get lost or damaged in the cafeteria? Yes, but not as many as I would have thought. I always allowed students to drop off their books at the classroom on their way to the playground, and some chose to stay in the classroom and finish whatever they were reading.

Here's the point: never waste time. There is so much waiting during fire drills, assemblies, cafeteria lines, and other school interruptions. It only took a few weeks, and suddenly all of my students and their friends in other classrooms would have something to read with them at all times.

2 Readers' Theatre

My friend and colleague Tim Rasinski is one of the world's foremost authorities on reading fluency, and he advocates (as do I) that Readers' Theatre is one of the best ways to build students' reading fluency. I would also argue that it is a great strategy for getting students excited about reading. For Readers' Theatre, students read aloud directly from scripts without props or costumes or sets.

Readers' Theatre provides students with the opportunity to "perform" what they read, thus enlivening text. Give students a piece of writing on Monday (you can differentiate the degree of difficulty on a student-by-student basis), and students must practice reading their piece daily until their grand performances on Friday before their classmates or invited guests (e.g., parents, other classes, community members, etc.). Through repeated readings, Rasinski and others have found that students' reading confidence builds on each subsequent reading of a piece. This, in turn, affects how well students identify words, read with meaning, and provide expression to what they read. As a result, students do not sound like robots but rather can read familiar pieces fluidly without interruption. By allowing students to perform their pieces, teachers can ensure that students will take the exercise seriously and practice as much as necessary.

Students can use a variety of different types of pieces for Readers' Theatre, including poetry, speeches, dialogues, commercials, movie trailers, chants, song lyrics, and parodies, to name a few. Using the Internet, teachers can find transcripts of all kinds of different reading passages.

3 Guided Reading

Don't get me wrong: I like guided reading. I believe that teachers need to present reading materials of various difficulty levels throughout the day and encourage students with varying abilities to work together. Guided reading is also essential for grouping students of similar abilities to help them succeed at reading a text they can manage. Essentially, guided reading is an approach that allows teachers (or more proficient readers) to work with a small group of students to help them learn effective strategies for processing text with understanding. Guided reading allows students of varying reading levels to better understand how more proficient readers process texts.

While I like guided reading, I view it as a routine, and I have a philosophy about routines. If I model anything repeatedly, there is no reason why students cannot take the reins and lead that routine on their own. Therefore, after a month or two of leading guided reading groups, I used to turn control over to different students to run my guided reading groups while I worked individually with different students.

Thinking aloud and questioning are the thrust of any successful guided reading experience, so I trained my students to follow a five-step process when participating in a guided reading (the number of steps does not matter; use whatever works best for your students):

1. Set the scene (discuss cover and title).

2. Do a picture walk (students look only at pictures and guess story).

3. Read the text together (partner read).

4. Respond to the text.

5. Return to the text. Allow students to read pages aloud individually.

While many teachers think they have to lead their guided reading groups, I often let students lead mine. I did not always use students from my class, mind you. For example, when I taught second grade, I frequently asked fourth- and fifth-grade teachers to send me some of their struggling students to help my struggling students. What we found is that the older students would improve their reading along with the younger ones, and all students' behavior improved when working together. The sequence is basic enough that it can be taught to parents and older siblings, as well, so I often trained volunteers to work with my students.

QUICKIE STRATEGY: BRAINSTORMING

Brainstorm. Brainstorm. Brainstorm. It is essential to survey students constantly about their background knowledge because instruction begins where students are, not at the front of the curriculum guide.

4 Choral Reading

There is strength in numbers. I was blessed to teach a lot of ESL students who had emigrated from various countries. No matter what class or age level that I have taught, however, there has always been a huge discrepancy in ability levels and interests. Some kids like to talk, and others do not make a peep until well into the class term. By giving students daily routines during which they all read together, teachers can facilitate a lively classroom where all students feel like they are participating and improving.

I never compared students to one another. I preferred to compare them to their own prior performances. Choral reading is a great way to encourage students to participate because the untrained ear cannot detect which students are "faking it" when the entire class reads aloud together.

With young children especially, try to engage students with predictable text. Translation: sing lots of songs and read lots of poems and nursery rhymes. The predictability helps all students who are trying to learn how to read, especially those who do not speak English at home. I used a lot of poetry, songs, and nursery rhymes because while many students may not be able to read different pieces per se, they may have them memorized. The simple act of reciting them aloud is a great motivational tool to boost students' reading confidence. One of the reasons I love Dr. Seuss (or, as my little ones used to call him in Spanish, Dr. "Je-Seuss") is because his stories always rhymed, and that predictability is very reassuring to beginning and struggling readers. Shel Silverstein is another popular author students appreciate.

5 Thematic Reading

When I was a kid (back when there were still black and white televisions, and people had to get out of their seats to turn a channel), CBS used to make made-for-TV movies about a variety of subjects, like the Mercury astronauts. At the end of the movie, the star actor from the movie would come on-screen and announce, "If you enjoyed this movie about the Mercury astronauts, here are 20 books you can get about them that can be found at your local library." I think one of the best ways to enhance students' reading vocabularies is to introduce them to the same words in a variety of contexts. That's what I like most about thematic reading.

No matter what we were learning in school, I tried to tie everything around a similar theme. I'd go to the library and check out a number of books related to that theme (in case you did not know, most libraries will offer teachers special library cards that enable them to check out a greater number of materials). While some students may not be interested in a fictitious story about hurricanes, they may find a nonfiction text intriguing. Creating libraries around a theme is a way to differentiate instruction for students while meeting their various readiness levels and interests.

Thematic reading also lends itself to artifacts for building student interest. For example, when I taught first graders about oceans, I brought in seashells, created centers with plastic storage boxes filled with beach sand for students to write in, and set up a machine that made wave sounds. Then I'd supply a variety of picture books, chapter books, magazine and newspaper articles, poems, encyclopedia entries, and other materials for students to read in our classroom library. I'd also encourage students to write their own pieces for inclusion in our various thematic libraries. I tried to build my classroom curricula around a different theme every three to four weeks.

6 Reward Students with Reading Time

Kids are not stupid. They know that if you have to bribe them to read, then it's probably not worth doing on their own. I mean, I am happy that Pizza Hut sponsors the Book It! program to get students reading, but I would suggest one modification to the program. The way it currently works is students read lots of books and get rewarded with pizza. I'd do it the other way: I'd reward students for eating pizza by giving them books. It is a subtle difference, but a big one. I wanted to make reading a reward in itself for students, and I had a number of tricks up my sleeve.

I used reading as motivation. When my students were doing a good job at something, I promised that "we'll earn another read-aloud if we finish this activity in the next 10 minutes." I rewarded students with extra free-reading time or promised them we would read outside. On Fridays, if my students had successfully completed our class goals for the week, I would read to them while they lay down on the floor on pillows they had brought in anticipation of "Fluffy Fridays." I tended to read aloud books like Mark Twain's *Tom Sawyer* or Roald Dahl's *Matilda* or Jules Verne's *20,000 Leagues Under the Sea*. The possibilities are endless.

What can you do to get students viewing reading as a rewarding activity? One thing I know for sure: your presentation matters. I have heard some teachers whose read-alouds put me to sleep, and other teachers who can thrill their students about "going on bear hunts" or "searching for lost treasure." Again, students usually value what the teacher values, so if you are the kind of teacher who shows kids that "reading time is happy time," the kids will inherit that attitude.

QUICKIE STRATEGY: INDIVIDUAL PROGRESS

Celebrate students' growth by focusing on each student's individual progress. Allow students at the end of the day to reflect on their day's accomplishments, who helped them with their reading, and who they helped with reading in class.

7 Get Students Library Cards

A lot of people are not aware that the government has a program that you can find in just about every community. They have these buildings, and in these buildings are rows and rows of books. Now, you apply for this free card, and these institutions will let you take books home for up to three weeks in most cases. They're called "public libraries," and they provide access to the greatest knowledge in the world for free. For many parents and students, I also point out that public libraries have these things called "books on tape" for those who claim they do not know how to read.

Yes, my father was a public librarian. No, I did not like libraries. On the contrary, I thought public libraries were smelly, creepy places where old ladies told you to be quiet, the furniture was uncomfortable, and a freak always snuck around the book stacks acting like a vampire. Still, I grew up privileged because every night my father brought home tons of books to share with my siblings and me. We may not have had a lot of money, but we always had a wealth of literature at our disposal.

I was appalled to learn that so many of my students and their parents had never visited the public library. They were literally wasting tax dollars by not utilizing one of the few things in government that pays back citizens. Do yourself a favor and ask your local library to send a representative to your school to register students and their families for library cards. I think there is no greater way to create a passion for reading than to introduce students to all the resources our libraries have to offer. And one final note: the children's librarians are usually awesome.

8 Closed-Captioning

When I trained the parents of my students at bimonthly workshops (when I was teaching elementary school, I used to hold workshops every other Friday to assist parents in helping their children academically at home), one of our discussion points was the number of reading materials in the home. One of the strongest indicators of how well a student is going to perform in school is the number of books present in the home. Since a lot of my parents claimed to be poor and not have much money for books, I searched for ways to introduce reading materials into their homes. One of the best resources is present in just about every home in America: television.

Less than 20 years ago, Congress passed a law that required every television set in this country to have closed-captioning (text for the hearing impaired). I always tell parents that even if they have nothing else to read in their homes, I can predict that they probably have a television set. If they do nothing else, parents should turn on the closed-captioning feature on their television sets so students see print on the screen as they watch their programs.

Now, a lot of people point out to me that if the television programs are in English and the subtitles are in English, what good does that do? That is a fair point, and here is another one: have you ever tried to watch a program with subtitles and not look at the subtitles? That is a pretty tricky thing to do.

I am not a believer in inundating students or their parents with a lot of nightly homework. About 30 minutes per night is sufficient. One of our jobs as teachers is to help educate parents on steps they can take to help their children become better readers, and—in my experience—parents are thrilled when they learn about closed-captioning. It is an easy activity that can have a positive effect on their children's reading attitudes and aptitudes.

QUICKIE STRATEGY: DAILY READING TIPS

Allow students to provide testimonials on a daily basis of strategies they use while they read. It is important for students to recognize one another's different learning styles and how they deal with adversity when reading.

9 Get Students on Free Mailing Lists

Speaking of parents who claim to have nothing to read at home, I'd like to point out another trick that I introduced to teachers and also parents at my workshops to help influence the reading environment at home.

There are two types of people in this world, problem solvers and excuse makers. My advice to you is to stay away from the excuse makers and don't let them bring you down. I was once training some first-grade teachers who sat around a table and whined:

"You don't understand, we teach the poor kids!"

"Our kids don't speak English!"

"They've got nothing to read at home!"

After listening to one complaint after another and feeling the positive energy draining from my body, I took these teachers on a field trip to the local bookstore. We walked over to the magazine racks, and I showed them the travel magazine section, where we began to remove some of the loose index cards from the magazines. The next day we helped the first graders fill out the cards and mail them. Three weeks later the kids were asking one another, "Which cruise are you going on, Sylvia? The Caribbean or the Alaska cruise?" Sure, to adults this kind of mail can be an annoyance, but young children love getting mail. I have yet to see a third-grade boy who receives 20 brochures a day and feels resentful. They love it.

Don't stop there. Get the students on catalog mailing lists and pick up or subscribe to museum or lecture schedules, free neighborhood or regional newspapers, entertainment guides, free real estate magazines, and free classified advertising magazines/newspapers.

I made sure that my students sent away queries for college applications. I wanted students to see all of the free resources that were available to all of them.

QUICKIE STRATEGY: COUNTDOWNS

Facilitate "countdowns" with students. After reading passages, ask students to focus on 3-2-1: three things they learned from a reading, two things they found to be interesting, and one question they have.

10 Celebrity Readers

Keep in mind that a lot of parents do not come to school for student events because they had a lot of negative experiences when they were in school. To me the single most important partner I had in education was the parent of each of my students, and I needed to do whatever it took to get that person on my side. So, I did whatever I could to promote parent involvement, and one of my simplest tricks was to train my students to treat every parent like he is a celebrity.

Whenever a parent of one of my students walked into my classroom, my students would immediately hop from their seats with pencils and papers in hand and hound that parent for an autograph. I ask you, if you visited a place where all the kids treated you like a rock star, would you feel hostile or become more inclined to visit that place again? In my experience, parents loved coming to our classroom because they always felt appreciated.

Once you get the parents coming to your classroom, put them to work. I asked parents to read aloud to my students all the time (in fact, Wednesdays in my classroom used to be reserved for our "mystery readers," who were typically parents who would come in to read our final story of the day). If you are fortunate enough to have parents who can volunteer significant chunks of time, ask them to run guided reading groups or work one-on-one with struggling readers. Another tip I give parents who are frustrated that their child will not read with them: swap kids. I advise them to work with the child of their best friend and ask their friend to read to their child. The most important thing is to let students know that reading is important to everybody.

11 Context Clues

We know that average students learn 3,000 to 4,000 words each year. If that's the case, that means even someone who graduates at the bottom of his high school class has at least 36,000 words in his working vocabulary. He could not have learned all of those words from vocabulary quizzes. If he took a 20-word vocabulary quiz every week from kindergarten through high school, he would have more than 10,000 words in his vocabulary. So where did he develop the rest of that vocabulary? He did what Sherlock Holmes did: he searched for clues.

When students read, they constantly use familiar words and context to determine new word meanings. With young students I demonstrate this with real word exercises. With adults (who have much more sophisticated vocabularies), I must make the point using nonsense words. Read the following examples:

poliath

Tyson hates Fridays because his teacher always gives his class a poliath.

What is a poliath? How did you know? I am guessing that you determined it is a test based on your prior experiences, but sometimes you must see a word a couple of times before you are truly sure of its meaning, like with "wamzerger":

wamzerger

The other day I was at the mall when I saw a clown playing with a wamzerger. The wamzerger was bright blue and floated above his head. He attached his wamzerger to a string and tied it around his wrist so he would not lose it. The clown and I hit the wamzerger back and forth until my mom told me to go with her.

What is a wamzerger? Which sentence gave it away? I am guessing that you probably determined a wamzerger is a balloon, and you figured it out in the second sentence. In the first sentence you saw the word "clown" and drew a picture of a clown in your brain, but it was the word "floated" in the second sentence that confirmed your prediction. Sometimes, though, words take several exposures to learn, like "cacojar":

cacojar

The cacojar is down the street from Valerie's house. Sometimes she goes there with her mother. There are always lots of people standing in line, and the cacojar workers take a long time helping people. Valerie's mom says she would rather not go to the cacojar, but she needs to buy stamps.

I bet you determined a cacojar is a post office, and you figured it out when you read the word "stamps." What's my point? Teach students how to use context cues to determine new vocabulary words, and reading can be a challenging, fun, and rewarding activity.

12 Reading Counts

I am not a big fan of incentives, and I'll tell you why: most reading incentives send the wrong messages to kids.

Teachers always ask me if I think the Accelerated Reader (AR) program is bad (AR is a daily progress monitoring software assessment used in many schools to monitor students' reading progress), and I give my standard answer: it depends. I am not opposed to anything that attracts otherwise reluctant readers to reading. I do not, however, support any program that is mandated as "the" way. There is only one reading method that works for all students, and that is my method: variety. You have to arm yourself with lots of weapons of mass instruction in your teaching arsenal because what works for this kid might not work for that kid; what works in first period may not work in fifth period; what works this year may be a disaster next year. To me, reading incentives should focus on reading as a reward in itself.

Some of my students liked to compare the sizes of the books they read, the number of books read, the different types of books they read, etc. I tried to offer different ways to keep track, but none really mattered to me. All that mattered is that I got each student excited about reading, and I would adapt to whatever worked for that particular child. For example, when I was a kid my teacher used these "S.R.A." kits that were different colors. (SRA Reading Mastery is a reading program that's been around forever, and SRA stands for "Science Research Associates.") There were always annoying kids in the class who would boast they were "reds" while I was stuck on "blue." One day I discovered the expression "So?," and labels never bothered me again when they were applied to me.

I really wanted my students to focus on reading as the reward, but I did cave from time to time and promoted how much my students read. My best suggestion is for teachers to go to a handicraft store, purchase a bead kit for about $14, and reward students for reading with beads. I gave all of my second graders plastic necklaces and would give them a bead for every book they read (I later modified the system based on time spent reading, which to me is a better habit to focus on). My students would walk around the classroom wearing their necklaces while classmates admired how many beads they had earned. Use whatever works.

QUICKIE STRATEGY: ACTIVE LISTENING

Encourage students to become active listeners. When asking the entire class a question, allow students to discuss their answers with a partner first.

13 Graphic Organizers

A lot of students prefer to analyze reading information visually. As I worked with a lot of ESL students, I tried to present information in the form of graphic organizers to ensure that students comprehended what we had read about.

Venn diagrams are great because they allow students to compare and contrast the similarities and differences between characters, settings, stories, and a host of other things. Teachers and students can display information with words and phrases or even pictures.

I am also a big fan of K-W-L Plus charts, because they allow students to think about topics throughout the reading process. Students share what they know about a topic, what they'd like to know, what they learned from what they read, and what they still want to learn that they did not learn from their reading (K = Know, W = Want to know, L = Learned, Plus = What they still want to know).

K-W-L Plus   Independence Day

K What We Know	W What We Want to Know	L What We Learned	Plus What We Still Need to Learn
(5) fireworks (5) picnics (3) Constitution (2) Liberty Bell (1) Independence Hall (4) Paul Revere (3) Declaration of Independence (4) Benjamin Franklin (4) George Washington (4) Thomas Jefferson (1) Lexington and Concord (5) parades (2) American flag (2) Statue of Liberty (6) July 4, 1776	Why do we celebrate Independence Day on the Fourth of July? What is the Declaration of Independence? Why do we have fireworks on the Fourth of July? Why did the colonies want to declare independence? Who led the first Continental Army?	Thomas Jefferson was the main writer of the Declaration of Independence. America said it was independent from Britain with the Declaration of Independence. The Continental Congress signed the Declaration of Independence on July 4, 1776, in Philadelphia in Independence Hall. The 13 colonies voted to become 13 independent states of the United States of America. Benjamin Franklin, Thomas Jefferson, and many others signed the Declaration of Independence.	Were any other countries involved in the American Revolution? How come the first American flag had only 13 stars? For how long did we keep fighting the British after we signed the Declaration of Independence? Does any other country have a Declaration of Independence? Why was the Declaration of Independence signed in Philadelphia?

Categories of Information We Expect to See:
1. landmark
2. symbol
3. essential document
4. historical figure
5. celebration activity
6. important date

Vocab-O-Grams, also known as "Predict-O-Grams," allow students to make predictions about how authors use particular words to tell a story. Vocab-O-Grams are used with a charting process that asks students to organize vocabulary in relationship to the structure of the selection. For example, I used to write a list of target vocabulary words on an overhead projector and asked students to discuss what they knew about the words. Next, I would pass out Vocab-O-Gram handouts to groups of four students and asked each group to predict where each vocabulary word could be found as it related to the story structure (so students would place the

Vocab-O-Gram

Click, Clack, Moo: Cows That Type by Doreen Cronin

New Vocabulary Words

* Farmer * Barn * Problem * Impossible * Type * Electric	* Strike * Closed * Busy * Note * Cows * Eggs	* Furious * Typewriter * Party * Emergency * Snooped * Exchange

Setting Barn, farmer, cows, eggs	**Which words tell you about when and where the story took place?** on a farm
Characters Farmer, cows, eggs, busy, furious	**Which words tell you about the characters in the story (their feelings, thoughts, appearance)?** There is a farmer, cows, and something that lays eggs on the farm. Someone is busy, and someone is furious.
Problem/Goal Problem, strike, emergency, typewriter	**Which words describe the problem or goal?** There is an emergency strike on the farm. Someone uses a typewriter.
Action Type, note, closed, snooped, exchange, deal	**Which words tell you what might happen?** Maybe someone types a letter to offer a deal in exchange for something.
Resolution Party, deal	**Which words tell you how the story might end?** Maybe they have a party once they have a deal.
What questions do you still have?	If the story is about typing cows, why are there eggs? What is the problem with cows that type?
Mystery words	Impossible, electric (probably deals with typewriter)

words "village" under "setting"), and we would discuss if students predicted correctly after reading a story. I have found that students, especially my ESL students, would really benefit from seeing how target vocabulary words are used throughout a selection.

A variety of different graphic organizers exists to help enhance students' vocabulary and comprehension skills. Whichever you choose, the point is to make reading materials more accessible to students and solidify their understanding of whatever is being read in class.

14 Classroom Library Checkout

I ran my classroom library the same way I tried to run most systems in my class: I trained my students how to run it, and then I let them run it. I learned a long time ago that the secret to being a successful teacher is the secret to all positions of leadership: be a servant leader. By that I mean that I always appreciated and valued the thoughts and talents of all my students, and I got out of their way as much as possible. To me, education works best when students discover things for themselves.

People ask me if students damaged our classroom library. I will warn you now to expect some spills in your library, and the books will sometimes be misfiled. You can also expect to lose nearly 20 percent of your books each year, due to wear and tear and the occasional wandering title. I can also predict that your students, once given the responsibility to take care of their own library, will take that responsibility very seriously. As a matter of fact, as neat and organized as I like to be, I learned that my students could be even more so when it came to managing our classroom library.

I am a big fan of homeowners over renters. Why? Homeowners generally take better care of their lawns. The same principle holds true in a classroom. I know it's difficult for a lot of teachers to hand over control of systems to their students, and, believe me, young students do not master systems quickly. Over time, however, I believe that your students will learn more by being given responsibilities than by being told to be responsible. Additionally, allowing students to run the classroom library and ensuring that they take care of their library teaches students the value of books, an added bonus.

QUICKIE STRATEGY: USING RUBRICS

Use rubrics to allow students to clearly see what is expected of them when they read.

15 Jigsaws and Component Parts

One way to boost student interest in reading is to facilitate student "jigsaw" teams. Teachers run jigsaws in various ways, and I switched mine from time to time. Generally, my students used to sit at tables in teams of four, and each table member was assigned a responsibility. While all students read the entire passage, different students had different assignments to pay attention to (e.g., if you asked your four friends to drive your car and tell you what they thought, you could ask all of your friends to give you an overall impression. You might ask one to tell you how smooth the ride was, another to talk about the car's amenities, another to describe how comfortable the space was, and another to discuss how visually appealing the car was). I liked to use a large responsibility wheel on a bulletin board with four clear colors, and each color had a different responsibility pinned to it. Each table member had a color, and her color decided her responsibility. For example, if we were focusing on point of view, each person would have the responsibility of thinking through the eyes of a different character from the story. Sometimes I would assign each member a different story element to focus on (e.g., setting/characters, problem, action, resolution).

Think of jigsaws like a car game. When I was a kid and my parents took my brother, sister, and me on long road trips, they would play games with us that concentrated on different things we could see from our windows. For example, my brother Jim would look for numbers, my sister Liz would look for letters, and I would look for restaurants (I was the chunky one with a large appetite). In the same way, jigsaws add an extra component of interest that draws added student attention. I have seen some teachers turn jigsaws into a competition between different teams. Whatever works for you is fine, as long as it builds student interest in reading.

QUICKIE STRATEGY: KEY TERMS

Preview topics by introducing students to key terms. Johnny Carson used to play a character on *The Tonight Show* called "Carnac the Magnificent." Carnac was a psychic who would visualize a few key words and phrases and then open an envelope to reveal the question to the answers he had previously given. Encourage students to concentrate on terms and pay attention to how they are used in passages and what they mean.

CHAPTER 4

Writing

Writing? I thought this was a book on reading. Well, it is, and good teachers recognize that reading and writing are reciprocal processes. It is also important for early elementary school teachers to realize the range of writing skills that are present in their classrooms.

Every class of young students I have ever taught essentially had three types of writers. At the low end of the spectrum were my emergent writers. During this stage, children will begin with random marks or scribbles, and move toward discovering that scribbling and drawing can represent something. For example, I saw a student write "I LK HKP," and her teacher read it as, "I like housekeeping." Hooray! Whenever I see a teacher who can correctly decipher "I like housekeeping" from "I LK HKP," I marvel. That teacher reminded me of Indiana Jones, who can effortlessly decipher Sanskrit on any stone tablet. These teachers just blow me away.

While a lot of my younger students were emergent writers, there were some who were evolving to beginning writers. During this stage, children begin to write in a more conventional way. Their writing becomes more readable, by themselves and by others. For example, a student may write "My gamnomen cam to my hosn." Read aloud, this child's writing may sound like German, but even I can translate what this child means.

Finally, I usually had a few transitional writers in my class, too. During this stage, children write with increasing fluency and expression. They express their ideas in more complex ways, and they are able to write with greater speed. They are able to present a sequence of events, and stories have morals. For example, a child may write "My cousin came from Alaska for the holidays. She came to school with me for two days! Then we had a happy chismas. The day after chismas I siting in a car going to Disnyland!" While the child may be infatuated with exclamation points and misspell a word or two, she is writing quite well.

A teacher recently asked me if all good readers are good writers. I told her that was not necessarily true, but I did assure her that all good writers are good readers. I have never met a student or adult who was a good writer but not an avid and proficient reader. By using writing we can stimulate students' interest and proficiency in reading.

1 Student-Created Materials

When I was first handed a class of young children, my principal gave me 33 students and two books. Fortunately, even though I taught at an under-resourced school, we had a lot of construction paper and a laminating machine. I challenged my students to create their own library, and in just six weeks, my 33 students had written over 400 books.

Now, these books varied from student to student. Llesenia turned in a 30-page book on the history of everything, while José turned in a six-page book called *Mi Familia, por José*. When you opened up the book, one page had a stick figure drawing with the words "Mi Papá" etched below it, followed by the next page with a similar sketch and the words "Mi Mamá" and additional pages with "Mi Hermanita," "Mi Perrito," and "El Fin." On the back of each book I placed an author biography with a photo of the author

(I had placed the students in groups of three, taken their photos, and cut out their heads). A typical biography would read something like: José Cardenas is the author of *Mi Familia (My Family)*, *Mi Escuela (My School)*, and the very popular *Mis Amigos (My Friends)*. He lives in Compton, California, with his family. He enjoys soccer and spaghetti. When he grows up, he wants to be a police officer.

José taught me a lot about the power of student-created reading materials. First of all, despite being almost a non-reader, José could read all of the biographies on the back covers of student-created books. Why? He was interested in his classmates. He had memorized a lot of the biographies, but that was a critical step in his literacy development. Second, José became an avid writer because he had an ego and enjoyed seeing his photograph on the backs of books. He wrote over 40 books: *Mi Cabeza (My Head)*, *Mis Zapatos (My Shoes)*, and *Mi Pelota (My Ball)*. It was ridiculous. Third, José learned to take care of books because he knew if he messed up Laretta's book, she would beat him up at recess (one of the joys of teaching young children is discovering that the boys are often fearful of the girls).

I learned that writers are readers. Writing became a useful tool in my quest to engage my students in reading.

QUICKIE STRATEGY: INDEX CARDS

Write words on index cards to review the concept of words with emergent writers. Give the cards to students, and have each student recite his words in an oral sentence.

2 Silly Questions

I do not like idle students. Let me correct myself: I fear idle students. Idle students inevitably disrupt other students and cause all sorts of other mischief, so I used to seek ways to occupy my students constantly. One of my students' optional activities after they completed whatever activity we were working on was to create silly questions.

The way silly questions work is like this: when a child finishes an activity early, she can write (or draw or scribble, depending on her degree of literacy) on a small note card a silly question to ask either the teacher, a character, or a puppet. ("Characters" are people I acted like to capture my students' attention, e.g., Australian Pete, Grumpy Old Man. I also used puppets to answer a lot of students' questions.) At the end of our school day, once we had completed all of our learning goals for the day, one of my students' free choice options was to have their silly questions answered. I found this to be a great motivational tool to get students reading and writing more.

Students' typical questions went like this: "Mr. Brassell, when are you going to trim your nose hairs?" "This afternoon," I would say while covering my nose. "Thank you for bringing that to my attention, Luis." I learned very quickly that if you are going to teach young children, prepare to have thick skin because children do not have a lot of tact. From the mouths of babes comes brutal honesty. Just ask the emperor who had no clothes.

Between writing questions, asking their buddies to help them write questions, and discussing questions, my students covered a variety of language-arts standards in a fun, meaningful, and memorable way.

3 Sniglets and Morphemic Analysis

I will date myself. Back in the 1980s there used to be this wonderful show on HBO called *Not Necessarily the News*, and one of my favorite segments on the show featured comedian Rich Hall presenting his favorite "sniglets." According to Hall, sniglets are words that are not in the English language but should be. A variation of this activity that I used with students to enhance their vocabularies was called "Morphemic Analysis," in which students take prefixes, suffixes, and root words to create new terms. Morphemic Analysis sounds so formal, though, and sniglets have much more versatility.

For example, using Morphemic Analysis, my third graders once created the word "preteachology." Preteachology is the study of educating students before one knows what he is doing. I like to think they were not referring to me.

Sniglets, on the other hand, are not bound by any rules. Any letter combination can become a word, like the one the fourth grader creates in Andrew Clement's wonderful book, *Frindle*. The best sniglet I ever received from a first grader was the word "minutater." LaShonda, a six-year-old child, came up with minutater. Do you want to know what it means? Whenever you order french fries at McDonald's, have you ever noticed that one french fry is smaller than all the others? That french fry is the "minutater." I have to tell you that I may have been prouder and more impressed by LaShonda's minutater than anything I ever thought of. She had me howling with laughter.

Not all of your students will come up with words as clever as minutater, but that really does not matter. Sniglets allow students to play with language, which is a great way to enhance their literacy skills. One of the joys of reading Dr. Seuss books, for me, is finding nonsense words he creates in order to rhyme his stories. I encourage students to do the same.

4 Recipes and Cookbooks

My students loved bringing recipes to class. This is a great way to involve families in their children's literacy development. I encouraged parents to share recipes all the time with their children because cooking can be a great bonding experience for parents and children. Recipes, by nature, demonstrate the importance of reading directions and how reading functions in everyday life. Every family has a recipe, and I often got parents to come to our classroom to share their recipes with us.

If students do not have recipes, let them create their own special recipes. I still have a recipe I wrote in second grade that stood out from the rest of the class in that it was disgusting. Every other student, it would appear, interpreted the teacher's instructions to bring a recipe from home as sharing one of their mother's specialties. Students brought in intricate recipes for creating quiche, baking brownies, and making meatloaf. I wrote my own recipe for creating the world's most disgusting sandwich, deemed "the tuna and peanut butter special." Whenever I look at the class cookbook from my childhood, I am reminded that students see the world in different ways, and my job is to facilitate each student's development in any way I can.

After collecting students' recipes, you can assemble a class cookbook. Since my school did not have a copier that worked, I usually begged a local law firm to donate a couple of hours of time on their super-duper copy machine. Then I'd pass out cookbooks that included each student's recipe, and we would have a "cooking party" with parents where students and parents would autograph each other's cookbooks and feast together.

QUICKIE STRATEGY: CRAZIGRAMS

Encourage students to play with language by creating "crazigrams," which can take many forms. One students particularly enjoy is to take 10 letters and create a message (e.g., O U A T M B B A A W: Once upon a time my big brother ate a worm).

5 Mad Libs and Fractured Stories

Read my lips: kids love *Mad Libs*, the word game created back in the 1950s by comedy writers and wordaholics Leonard Stern and Roger Smith (www.madlibs.com). *Mad Libs* are stories missing important elements that are labeled by parts of speech, and the student's job is to fill in words for each missing part of speech. So if a person asks you for a number, a past tense verb, an adjective and a plural food, and you give 13, tripped, gorgeous and bananas, your *Mad Lib* might look something like this:

Once upon a time there were <u>13</u> bears who <u>tripped</u> in the forest. One day, the Mother Bear made a <u>gorgeous</u> pot of <u>bananas</u>.

While the writing activity might seem silly to most adults, I have had first graders pee their pants laughing because they loved *Mad Libs* so much. I used to have a student named Carlos who would work only if he received a signed order from the President of the United States. Reading, to Carlos, was as interesting as listening to radio static. Once I began giving Carlos *Mad Libs*, however, I saw a transformation that any home makeover show would envy. That boy could read and write *Mad Libs* for hours, and, after a while, he began creating his own *Mad Lib* books and sharing them with friends. Carlos could not contain himself when reading *Mad Libs*. He would point at me and say, "Isn't this hilarious? My goodness, this is the happiest day of my life!" How do you not love your job when you have a student who enjoys himself that much?

6 Lots of Poetry

I think poetry is the most underutilized resource available to teachers. If you want to develop a student's passion for reading, what better way than to introduce your students to poetry, a genre that combines the power, rhythm, and magic of words in various forms? I used to read aloud four poems a day to my students, and those four poems took less than 10 minutes of class time. I recited poems when students cleaned. I recited poems when students lined up. Students sat transfixed by the imagery of Cynthia Rylant, the playfulness of Jack Prelutsky, and the pain of Emily Dickinson.

I introduced my students to various forms of poetry, from basic rhymes to cinquains to acrostics to concrete poems. Students learned about the cultures behind limericks and haiku, and enjoyed playing with the structures of diamantes. When all else fails, I told students, write free verse because there are no rules for free verse.

One of my clever boys, Tyrell, proudly shared his mastery of poetry during one of our coffeehouse nights.

Every semester the students and I would dress in turtlenecks and berets, invite parents to the classroom, serve coffee, and perform our poetry at an "open microphone." During one of our poetry jam sessions, Tyrell stood before all our guests and carefully enunciated every syllable of his poem: "Recess," he said, staring intensely at his audience, "So cool." Then he made cow horn signs with both hands and announced, "Free verse." You've always got to keep an extra careful eye on the boys. Regardless, Tyrell and all of my students anxiously wrote and read as many poems as possible to excite parents at our coffeehouse nights.

7 Messages/Letters/ Notes

Get an empty photocopy paper box, stand it up vertically, decorate it with blue construction paper, and cut out a slot. Now you have a classroom mailbox. Students get a kick out of passing notes to one another in class. Rather than dismissing this as a disruptive activity, I encouraged my students to write to one another and place their messages and notes in envelopes and "mail" them to their classmates instead of passing notes directly. By formalizing the activity, we reviewed the formats of letters. Students also clamored to be the "letter carrier" of the day.

Once your students get the hang of it, match them with "pen pals" from other classes, and then watch them get into writing. If you really want students to write letters, believe me: there is a class in China that is just itching to write letters to your class. I never had a problem getting pen pals for my students in other countries. However, after I could not find a business to pay for the postage on our letters, I began using e-mail. While I do not like e-mail as much as actual letters (e-mail typically uses a much looser format), it is still a wonderful tool for encouraging students to read and write.

QUICKIE STRATEGY: HIDDEN BOOKS

Use word and picture cards to guide students to books, bookmarks, poems, etc. that you have hidden throughout your classroom (good activity for teaching students to follow directions).

8 Résumés and Job Applications

One of the things I try to encourage early elementary teachers to do is to bring back the fun play stations. Kids learn a ton by dressing up like firefighters and cooks, and they get a kick out of emulating grown-ups. Plus, they learn a lot of academic language in the process, which will serve them well.

A great way to interest students in reading is to get them looking at job postings, classified ads, job applications, and résumés. I used to ask different businesspeople from the community (if you need businesspeople in your classroom, start by asking service organizations like Rotary, Lions, Kiwanis, Elks, and Optimist clubs) to come to my class and talk about what they did and what kinds of jobs they offered. Before they would come to class, the students and I would research the guests' professions and what types of qualifications they needed to fill those positions.

Students would have prepared questions for our guests, and we each prepared a résumé to give to that person (no, I did not give the person my résumé, as I was perfectly happy to be teaching). I asked our guests to explain to my students what types of choices they would have to make in order to assume these different professional roles in society, but my students' questions were always much more interesting. Students would ask visitors what kinds of reading they had to do at their jobs, and when one guest mentioned he never read picture books at work, one confused boy asked me why we read so many picture books in school. (Students come up with some really good questions.) One guest looked at students' résumés and job applications and commented on the nice handwriting of one of my girls, Giselle. As a result, several boys began to take their time and use better penmanship from that time forward.

What I found by inviting guests to my classroom and asking students to review job applications and résumés was that more of my students became curious about how to get good jobs, how to market themselves better than other applicants, and why reading and writing matter.

9 Lists and Checkbooks

One of the best ways to get students interested in reading and writing is to show them how important these activities are in society. For example, you may tell students who are interested in baseball that even if they become baseball players, they will need to know how to read their contracts and any statements they have to make to their fans.

I engaged a lot of my students in writing by getting them to write grocery lists. Actually, lists of any kind will work. A lot of students like to write what they want for their birthdays or other holidays. I have never taught a class of young children that did not include at least one boy who liked to announce at the top of his lungs his top five favorites of any given thing, every day of the week.

"Mr. Brassell," Nestor would shout, "my favorite food today is pizza. Pizza was my third favorite food yesterday." Other times Nestor would list for me his favorite basketball players, colors, videogames, etc.

Every year I made a trip to area banks and asked for free checkbooks. My students loved writing checks to me and to one another. "Mr. Brassell, if you forget that I forgot to turn in my homework today, I will give you this check for one million dollars," Kyara said.

QUICKIE STRATEGY: PROVERBS AND ANALOGIES

Encourage students to finish proverbs and analogies. For example, give students the beginning of a proverb such as "You can lead a horse to water but. . .," and allow students to come up with their own ending. For analogies, encourage students to think creatively by comparing different objects, etc. (e.g., feet are to shoes as hands are to. . .).

10 Day Planners

From the first day of school I encouraged students to write down their goals in their day planners. Perhaps they had to dictate them to me at the beginning of the year, but every day I wanted my students to focus on what they wanted to accomplish and what they had to do to get there. I'd wander up to a student and ask, "Jonathan, what do you want to be when you grow up?"

"A banker."

"Really? Are you hanging out with bankers?"

When Jonathan shakes his head, I lean down and say, "Remember this: you usually turn out like the people you hang out with."

I would say that from day one. I wanted students to know that if they hung out with a bunch of basketball players, the chances are that they would play basketball. If they hung out with a bunch of smokers, they would probably start smoking. If they hung out with a bunch of kids with pink Mohawks who dress in black and think school stinks, they would probably turn out that way too. Written goals are essential, I reminded students, because they force you to pay attention to your behavior.

For example, I constantly battle my weight. I lose a lot of weight, but then it manages to find me again. Unless I write down my weight and what I eat every day, I slip into my old bad habits of overeating. Why? I grew up with a lot of people who overate and avoided healthy foods. As a result, I tell my students, I constantly have to struggle with my weight.

It is a lot tougher to break a bad habit than to develop a good one, so I want to emphasize to my little ones that they make decisions every day that will affect the rest of their lives. If that sounds heavy to tell a little kid, take a look at kids. I see young children watching too much television, playing too many videogames, and eating too much junk food—and people wonder why America has problems. Like I tell the teachers I train, if you do not like the parents of your students, just remember you are training 33 future parents. I want my students to set goals early and make themselves accountable for reaching those goals.

QUICKIE STRATEGY: WORD SEARCHES

Ask students to search for words in newspapers, magazines, and other readings that begin with certain letters, represent different parts of speech, etc.

11 Diaries and Student Voices

While day planners encourage students to set goals, diaries encourage students to reflect on their experiences. I wanted my students to constantly think about moments in their days. I wanted them to think about strategies that help and others that hurt. Diaries also allow students to express themselves (Gruwell 1999 and Masterson Elementary Students 2002), and a lot of my more hyperactive students appreciated writing in their diaries as a means of communicating frustrations to me.

Students' voices need to be heard. I reminded students that one of the best-selling books of the 20th century was written by a 12-year-old girl named Anne Frank. Children have a different way of viewing the world, and I believe getting students to write about themselves is a great way to get them interested in reading about others.

A lot of teachers tell me that they think diaries take too much time and reflect too much anger and sadness. Well, I guess that is one type of diary. One of the reasons I love teaching young children is they tend to be happier folks. You can encourage students to write diaries about comical experiences they have at school and home.

Another way I got students writing was by asking them to keep diaries as different characters from books. For example, I once asked a first grader to keep a diary as though he were a penguin. He was not writing conventionally yet, but he drew wonderful pictures in his diary and wrote random shapes that acted as his letters. When he dictated his diary to me, I wrote every word on his pages. It turned out that he was very happy being a penguin, but he was sick of eating fish all the time. He also wanted to know why he was a bird that could not fly. Observations like these are what made me love teaching so much.

QUICKIE STRATEGY: HOT DOG PHONOGRAMS

Step 1: Fold paper lengthwise, like a hot dog, and open it up.

Step 2: Fold bottom part of hot dog again into another hot dog and unfold it.

Step 3: Cut bottom part of hot dog into thirds (up to the center line).

Step 4: Fold bottom up again.

Step 5: Then fold over half of the top part of the hot dog.

Step 6: Staple bottom thirds into "pockets."

Step 7: Using strips of paper, create words that follow C-V-C (consenant-vowel-consonent) patterns.

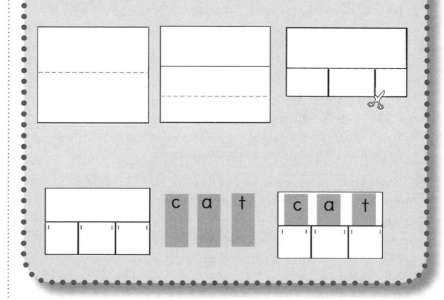

12 Hollywood Ending

A lot of my friends in Los Angeles are unemployed actors and actresses who have found their second calling as classroom teachers. I incorporated many of their ideas into my own classroom. I used to present myself to students as different "Hollywood" characters to encourage their reading and writing.

One way I encouraged students to write was to play "Hollywood Producer," acting like a fat cat with my pencil in my mouth and a constantly arched eyebrow. Whenever we read a story that had a sad or unsatisfying ending, I'd shout to my students in my best impersonation of Sam Goldwyn with my chin in the air, "That's not a very happy ending! Give me a happy ending!"

Students could rewrite endings on their own, with partners, or in small groups—whatever they preferred. I gave students a certain amount of time to rewrite the ending (sometimes half an hour, other times three days), and students would read aloud their endings to the class. After every student, pair, or group shared their ending, the rest of the class and I would act like studio executives and give the ending a "thumbs up" or "thumbs down." If an ending received a "thumbs down," I'd pat the writer or writers on the back and say, "Better luck next time," while the rest of the class echoed. Whatever endings received a "thumbs up" were written on the board and voted upon, and I gave the winning ending a Hollywood contract.

For some reason, my students and I always had a great time playing this game, but some teachers made the game ultracompetitive or negative for the losing writers. Don't fall into that trap. This should be a fun writing exercise that excites students about writing and encourages them to take risks.

13 Hollywood Movie Star

Tom Stoppard wrote the Academy Award-winning film *Shakespeare in Love*, but he is probably better known as a playwright. One of my favorite Stoppard plays is called *Rosencrantz and Guildenstern Are Dead*, where Stoppard takes the two smallest characters from Shakespeare's *Hamlet* and makes them the primary characters in his story. That inspired me to get my students to write themselves some juicy roles.

For Hollywood Movie Star I acted like the students' agent and told them that they needed to write a role that would give them as much publicity as possible. Students would take smaller characters from stories and make them primary characters in their versions of another story.

Another way to run this activity is for the teacher to act like a producer who wants to make as much money as possible. For example, I would tell my students to raise their hands if they liked *Harry Potter*, and all of my students would raise their hands. Then I would ask them to raise their hands if they enjoyed *Matilda*, and again, they all would raise their hands. Then I would act like a lightbulb had just lit up in my head and suggest to students, "Write me a story with Harry Potter and Matilda!"

It really doesn't matter how you run this activity. Again, the point is to encourage students' writing by suggesting alterations to familiar stories and characters. Once students realize they can play with story elements, you can lead discussions with students about different stories with similar elements.

14 Hollywood Rival

Here's a writing game my students loved: "Change an Element." My students and I would act like studio heads who were jealous that another studio had a hit. In a rush to capitalize on another studio's success, we'd copy their idea but add our own twist. Whenever we read a story, one of our comprehension activity options was to rewrite the story into students' environments. Students could change characters into their friends, make the setting their neighborhood, change the plot into something they'd experienced, etc.

For example, if I read aloud *Goldilocks and the Three Bears* to a group of first graders, students might work with partners or in small groups and change the story into "Samantha and the Three Big Brothers." In one of the students' stories (all pairs got an opportunity to read aloud their versions to the class), Samantha does not eat porridge; she eats Cheetos (regular, puffs, and flaming hot). After students rewrote the story, I would encourage them to share their versions with the entire class, and then they would lead a discussion on why they changed what they did, what they learned from their story, etc. It amazed me how the same students who thought Goldilocks was rude could find Samantha completely justified in eating her brothers' food without their permission. What

I liked most about allowing students to change elements in stories is that the activity let students reconsider previous notions about characters, settings, and plots and look at these elements from different points of view. I felt that students gained a much deeper understanding of stories by writing their own versions in this way.

QUICKIE STRATEGY: CLASS NEWSLETTERS

Create class newsletters, newspapers, invitations, and cards. Students read and write a lot more when they have an audience.

15 Hollywood Publicist

Comprehension activities do not have to be lame and tedious. Every day I read aloud at least one story to my students without showing them the cover of the book or telling them the title of the story. Acting like the head of a movie studio marketing department, I'd ask students to design a cover for the book and give the story a title. Students came up with some really cool covers and quite often came up with titles that were catchier than the stories in question.

This activity is easily differentiated. I have asked some students to draw covers and develop titles; other students also included a description of the book on the back cover; and some would write information in more than one language. Another

thing I would do was show students' covers and titles to other teachers' classes in our grade level and see if those students could guess what the story was.

QUICKIE STRATEGY: PAINT SAMPLE STRIPS

Give students paint sample strips. Paint strips usually progress from a dull color to a richer, darker color. Ask students to take a "dull" word (e.g., good) and create "richer" words for each progressive box (e.g., great, awesome, stupendous).

ames

Mary Poppins was right! Mary Poppins was an important educational philosopher of the 1960s who said something that continues to guide my teaching philosophy to this day: for every job that must be done, there is an element of fun. Translation: games are good. Make students think it's a game, and they are more likely to choose to do it on their own. I believe all of a teacher's reading strategies should be framed as fun activities in one form or another.

There are tons of books filled with vocabulary games, problem-solving games, writing games, spelling games, acting games, and plenty of other games that teachers can use to excite students about reading. The following strategies are meant to stimulate you to think about how to make reading a "game" for your students.

1 Performing as Book Characters

I hear a lot of talk about differentiated instruction in teacher preparation programs, and, ironically, most of the assignments we require our student teachers to complete are written. I think this is a big mistake because there are lots of ways to evaluate students' understandings of what they read.

Every class I have ever taught has some students who are a bit more outgoing than the rest of the class. These are the students who are so excited to answer questions and offer comments that they often shout before being called on or before raising their hands. I empathized with these students because I used to be one of them, so I tried to capture that energy and redirect it in productive fashions. One of the ways I allowed students to show the rest of us what they had grasped from what they had read was to let them dress up as characters from stories and re-enact them. We used to call this activity *Great Performances*, inspired by the PBS program of the same name.

At the beginning of the year, I would ask students to tell me what they watched on television. When they named a program, I challenged them to "prove it" by acting it out on their own or with their friends. Once students became familiar with this form of retelling, I encouraged them to use it as a means of demonstrating their understandings of different books we had read. While some students may have difficulties expressing their thoughts in writing, they may have little hesitation to perform. The point is to make the reading outcome an enjoyable experience so students are anxious to read and perform in the future.

2 Crosswords and Word Finds

I am a big believer in using games to teach students vocabulary words. Crosswords and word finds are two of my favorites.

One reason I love crosswords and word finds is because both are often included in daily newspapers. Once I point this out to students they realize that there is a new game that they can play every day in the newspaper. A lot of students do not realize all of the resources that are readily available to them. If you're like me, once you begin deciphering crossword puzzles you become addicted for life. There is a wonderful documentary film entitled *Wordplay* that chronicles compulsive crossword puzzle enthusiasts (including experts and celebrities).

I am going to demonstrate my age now. When I was an elementary teacher, we did not have the Internet to download quick and easy word finds. I used to have to create word finds from scratch on my own and run copies off on a mimeograph machine that left me with purple fingers every night. Nowadays, teachers can simply insert the number of words and the size of the puzzle they want to create, and the computer makes an instant word find. (A wonderful, free resource for teachers to create word finds can be found at www.puzzlemaker.com.) Teachers today have it easy! Did I mention I walked to school five miles uphill both ways?

Allow students to share their crosswords and word finds. You can even sponsor family night contests that match students with their parents and against them. I found that when I encouraged the use of crosswords and word finds with parents (and showed parents how to access them readily and for free), parents began to enjoy them almost as much as their children did. Like read-alouds, these times spent between parents and children produce positive results on students' enthusiasm for reading.

QUICKIE STRATEGY:
INTERACTIVE CAMPFIRE STORIES

Read aloud "interactive campfire stories," during which students make sound effects for different names and phrases (e.g., every time you read "cowboy," students say "yee haw").

3 Coded Messages

I liked to point out to students that language consists of random shapes, scribbles, and gestures passed down from one generation to the next. The symbols themselves are meaningless until the reader interprets them.

So why not allow your students to create their own "secret" languages? You can call this activity the "DaVinci Code" or whatever you like. Model how to create a language with your class. For example, maybe you decide to use the English alphabet, but each letter represents the next letter (e.g., "c" stands for "d" and "z" stands for "a"). Using this language you could challenge students to decode the message "Fnnc ktbj! (translated: Good luck!)"

With very young children I tended not to use the English letters, as many of these kids were having trouble enough as it was mastering our language. Instead we used pictures or numbers for each letter. Encourage students to work on their own, with a partner or in a small group, to create a language, and then they can create a coded message that the class has to try to interpret.

Once students got the hang of creating different "codes," I usually handed them different sentences to rewrite using their codes. Each sentence was a clue to where a hidden object was in the classroom, and I used this activity to get students to work together, look for patterns in writing, and problem solve. By paying attention to their various codes, students developed the ability to look for common features in print. I often used this activity in conjunction with lessons on prefixes, suffixes, and root words. You know it is a popular activity when students ask you to assign it as homework. Many students love to create messages for their parents to decode, too.

QUICKIE STRATEGY: OBJECT NAMING

An easy activity to facilitate daily with students (usually during transitions) is to write a letter on the board and ask students to name as many objects in the classroom that they can find that start with that letter.

4 Concentration and Memory Games

Give me a stack of index cards, and I can come up with about 500 different "Concentration" games. Concentration is simply a memory game. Students look at a set of cards placed upside down, and they get to turn over two cards at a time. The object is to pick out two matching cards; if the cards do not match, students place them back face down and let the next player take her turn. Meanwhile, all players concentrate on where they saw different cards in hopes of matching cards when it is their turn. When a player matches two cards, he gets to pick another two cards until the cards do not match.

You can create all sorts of variations of Concentration for your class, based on your students' various needs. I've created Concentration games where students match antonym-antonym, synonym-synonym, antonym-synonym, sight word-picture, Spanish-English, story element-specific story element from a book, present-past tense, capital letter-lowercase letter...the list goes on forever. This game is easy to differentiate, as you can add and subtract cards to match the degree of difficulty for the students.

The other thing I like about Concentration is that it is easy to show students and their parents how to make their own versions for home. I used to conduct parent workshops every other Friday in my classroom, and I would show parents how they could create the game with index cards, pieces of construction or writing paper, etc. It is also a great game because it can be used to reinforce students' understandings of concepts in all curricular areas, from reading/language arts to math/science.

QUICKIE STRATEGY: LAST-TO-FIRST

Last-to-First is a game in which a student says a word to another student (e.g., elephant), and that student must take the last letter from that word and think of a new word that begins with that letter (e.g., trampoline). Students who get stumped may ask a classmate for assistance.

5 Hangman or Guess the Word

When I was a kid I used to love when it rained because that meant our teacher would stay in the classroom with us, and we would all play "hangman." In the game of hangman, the teacher thinks of a word or phrase, draws a dash for each letter in the word or phrase, and then draws a picture of a gallows or noose. Students have to guess letters and try to determine the word or phrase that is on the teacher's mind. For each incorrect letter or guess, the teacher writes down the incorrect letter or guess and draws a different body part hanging from the noose. The goal is to guess the word before the complete stick figure is drawn and hanged. (I realize this may not be politically correct anymore, so here's a suggestion: avoid the gallows or noose! Just have students guess the word or phrase before the complete stick figure is drawn and give the game a different name.)

If you are teaching young children, you can use just about anything as subject matter. You could combine the idea of "hangman" with a different curricular concept that you would like to reinforce. For example, if my students were reviewing counting by 2s, 5s, or 10s and the missing word was "airplane," I would draw eight spaces for the eight letters and write out the progression starting with 2, 4, 6, and continuing out a ways. On each incorrect letter or guess, I would cross out a number (e.g., 2, 4, 6, 8, . . .) instead of drawing a part of a stick figure. If we were reviewing states, I'd use a map of the United States and shade in a state for each incorrect letter or guess. Students grew more and more excited to see how low a number or how few shaded states might accumulate before they could correctly solve each word puzzle. Basically, rather than adding a limb for each guess (which you still could do to review body parts), you use a different curricular item (and one that is not culturally sensitive).

If you are reviewing months of the year, draw the spaces for the letters of the word you're thinking about. Then write down all the months of the year and, for each incorrect letter or guess, cross out months starting with "January." See if the kids can guess the puzzle before you cross off "December." You can even pick a student to stand beside you, and each time students incorrectly guess a letter, ask that student to take one step to the left. See if the students can solve the word puzzle before the student has had to step sideways all the way out of the room! I've drawn stars, sung songs, added pieces of clothing to stuffed animals—be creative.

6 Board Games

Bring back the board games! Maybe I sound old-fashioned for saying this, but students can develop a variety of skills by playing board games. Alvin Rosenfeld said that "just by virtue of playing them, board games can teach important social skills, such as communicating verbally, sharing, waiting, taking turns, and enjoying interaction with others." I don't even bother teaching students the rules to many board games. Have you ever seen first graders play checkers? It is often like a scene out of *One Flew Over the Cuckoo's Nest*. My students could cover at least 20 state language arts standards by arguing over how to play the game, whose turn it was, and who won.

Board games are easily accessible, too. Some can be downloaded from the Internet. For the good, old-fashioned kind that I treasure, go to a local thrift store, and I am sure you can find 10 board games for $10. Discount stores sell a ton of them, too. You do not have to limit yourself to board games, either, as there are all sorts of card and travel games that I see for sale everywhere. I am sure they will hold the interest of the younger generation because McDonald's has had all sorts of success with its Monopoly promotions.

Board games do not have to mean "bored" games. Just because chess is an old game does not mean it is no longer magnificent. Students who play lots of board games develop their abilities to think creatively, problem solve, make predictions—sort of sounds like the habits of proficient readers, huh?

7 Author/Character Hot Seat

In my never-ending quest to provide students with multiple ways beyond book reports to demonstrate comprehension of what they read, one of the games I stumbled upon that delighted my students was the "Hot Seat" for characters and authors. This game basically resembles an oral, "thinking" person's book report.

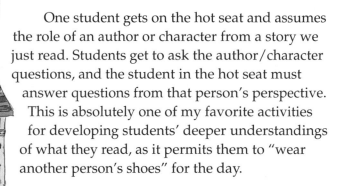

One student gets on the hot seat and assumes the role of an author or character from a story we just read. Students get to ask the author/character questions, and the student in the hot seat must answer questions from that person's perspective. This is absolutely one of my favorite activities for developing students' deeper understandings of what they read, as it permits them to "wear another person's shoes" for the day.

You can also use this activity as a means of checking to see if students have actually read certain books independently. I would often allow students to act like lawyers and "interrogate" the author/character to see if they could name story details. Students loved it when they could "bust" students who acted like they had read stories but could not recall details of what they read. We did this in good humor, but I wanted to make a point to students: good readers pay attention to details. Another great way to reinforce this skill is to read aloud a lot of mysteries to students to see if they pay attention to clues along the way. Then, as a class, we review how good authors drop hints and try to use those techniques in our own writing.

8 Idiomatic Expressions

Idioms are types of expressions whose meanings cannot be derived from the usual meanings of their parts. Since students frequently encounter idiomatic expressions in spoken and written discourse, teaching idioms is a useful strategy in exposing students to the meanings of such phrases. I used idioms to familiarize students with frequent expressions that cannot be defined by their literal meanings, allow students to realize the absurdity of idiomatic expressions' literal meanings, and provide links from the literal words to the nonliteral meanings to show students why figurative language is used in writing.

From a text I'd select some idiomatic expressions (e.g., the test was a piece of cake) and write them on the chalkboard. Then I'd ask students to draw pictures that illustrated the expressions and share their pictures with one another. Students would predict what each expression meant

as I wrote their various responses on the chalkboard. We'd read a passage from a text that used the idiomatic expression, and I would allow students to revise their definitions (if necessary) based on the expression's use in the text. For some students you may even ask them to write their own sentences that use the expressions. Students would discuss how they were able to determine the meanings of specific idioms from the context of the passage, and we would then examine three to five additional idiomatic expressions from the text.

Idioms are one of the trickiest things to understand in any language. English idioms can be particularly dauting. I always allowed my ESL students to work in partners and small groups to decipher the meanings of different idioms. Then I encouraged students to demonstrate their understandings in whatever ways they preferred, from pictures to skits, self-authored stories to greeting cards. Idioms lend themselves to a wide variety of differentiated products.

9 Bingo and Word Jumbles

I have a theory: when in doubt, create a bingo game. I created all sorts of bingo games for my students, but instead of shouting "bingo!" my students shouted "books!" (They both have five letters, get it? Cut me some slack, as it was late at night when I thought of that, and my students picked it up right away.) You can fill your bingo boxes with whatever you like: story elements, character names, favorite book titles, etc.

Another activity my students and I enjoyed were word jumbles, which you may find in newspapers across the country. Students are handed a bunch of letters and must arrange the letters in order to form a word. This is fun, but once students begin to get really good at word jumbles, challenge them to come up with anagrams. Anagrams are words or phrases that can be formed from other words or phrases. For example, from the word "teacher," students could come up with cheater, re-teach, act here, and a number of other possibilities. A Google search will turn up sites that will create anagrams from any words you enter.

Again, I use word games to teach students vocabulary, and I encourage them to play these at home. Host a parent night once a year for parents to come and learn how to play these games with their children. Invite other people from the community to attend as well. I invited lots of different businesspeople because I was constantly asking them to donate items to our classroom (e.g., I asked a carpet store owner to donate a reading carpet, a lawyer for time on his copy machine, a Kinko's manager for free binding for our class books; these are people who received invitations to all of our class events).

QUICKIE STRATEGY: STORY-STORY

For the story-story game, a small group of students creates a silly story together. Players must say and mimic three actions: they must take the last action the person before them said, make it into their own, and pass along a new action. For example, if the last thing a player said was "And I fell down," the next player would take, make, and pass their actions: "And I fell down, and I found a rock, and I put it in my pocket."

10 Magnetic Letters

I believe that a lot of students in this country learn to read and write by playing with magnetic letters on their refrigerators at home. If you do not have a refrigerator in your classroom, you probably could go to an auto shop and buy an oil tin for under $10. Oil tins are magnetic. Buy a can of white spray paint and make the tin into a whiteboard. You can get the magnetic letters from a discount store. There you go: you just made yourself a magnetic whiteboard (teachers are amazingly resourceful).

I like magnetic letters because students can manipulate them and create words in a fashion other than writing. If you don't have magnetic letters, write letters on index cards and give each student a set (obviously, it is a good idea to create multiples of certain letters, like vowels).

I also enjoyed using magnetic letters and index cards to try to get my students to remember information by incorporating as much movement as possible. For example, I taped letters on the tiles of the classroom floor and asked students to hop on letters to spell different words. You'd be amazed how much better children spell when movement is added. You can create poster boards with individual letters of the alphabet and ask teams of students to spell out different words (e.g., if you have five members on a team, give them five poster boards and five-letter words). You can even create laminated keyboards for students and ask them to "type" their words with their feet.

Another way we used magnetic letters or index cards with letters was to scramble up the letters and see how quickly students could spell out words with the scrambled letters.

11 Charades and TPR

Just because a student does not talk a lot in your classroom does not mean that student is not learning. Just because a student sits in the front row, has an answer or comment for everything, and envisions herself as a future congresswoman does not mean she is learning any more than the person sitting in the back of the classroom. In fact, I found that a lot of my quietest students who sat in the back and never said a word learned the most. A lot of my ESL students, in particular, who are quiet in class have a lot to say; they just cannot express themselves confidently in English yet.

Charades and other nonverbal activities allow students who are not eager to talk to still participate in class activities and demonstrate understanding. Again, I like charades mostly for their use of movement, as all learners (especially young ones) benefit from getting up out of their seats frequently.

Back in the early 1980s researcher James Asher developed an approach to language acquisition that he called "total physical response," or "TPR" for short. While I appreciate the approach, I hate the jargon. Here is what it means in terms a person like me can understand: play "Simon Says" with your students. You can even allow students to lead the activity and read different instructions to their classmates. By incorporating motions, teachers can differentiate various reading comprehension activities and facilitate active, thoughtful participation that does not require as much vocabulary for ESL students.

12 Beach Ball Learning

Give me a beach ball from a discount store, and I can teach my young students just about every standard in the curricula. Get your students out of their seats, form a circle, and bounce or toss the beach ball among students. Label your beach ball with whatever concept you would like to review. For example, if you want to review phonemic awareness, you can write various letters and blends on the ball and have students make the sound of the letter or blend that their right hand touches when catching the ball. I've colored various sections of beach balls before and asked students to review concepts like story elements, writing traits, proficient reader habits, and parts of speech based on the color their left hand touched.

You can use beach balls for just about anything. Partially inflate them and use them as seat cushions to allow some of your more active students to move around without leaving their seats. Toss the beach ball to different students and ask them about their favorite books, characters, and genres. Challenge a student to blow up a beach ball while another student reviews the sequence of important events in a story before the ball is fully inflated. Ask volunteers to kick the beach ball at various books to determine the next read-aloud story. Slowly deflate a beach ball while small groups search for target vocabulary words in stories, and see if they can find the five to seven words before the beach ball is completely deflated. If you cannot think of ways to use beach balls, ask your students. They will constantly provide you with brilliant ideas.

13 Songs and Chants

I probably love using songs and chants more than any other activity to assist my students in learning to read, loving learning, and remembering information. I'll bet it's because songs and chants have always had a way of sticking in my head.

I can prove the value of songs and chants. Who was the 18th President of the United States? How many bones are in the human body? How many voting members of Congress are there? (If you really must know: Ulysses S. Grant, 206, and 535 voting members of Congress)

If you had trouble with those, let's see if you can complete any of these:

"In fourteen hundred and ninety-two…"

"Plop, plop—fizz, fizz…"

"Conjunction, junction…"

(In case you missed them: "Columbus sailed the ocean blue," "Oh! What a relief it is," and "What's your function?")

Someday you may have Alzheimer's and not remember the names of your own children, but you'll be able to remember jingles you learned when you were a six-year-old. That's how kids remember the English alphabet—by learning it to the tune of "Twinkle, Twinkle, Little Star."

My students and I created songs and chants every single day in our classroom. We would sing a variety of songs and chants that covered different objectives. For example, to learn shapes:

Circle *(to the tune of "If You're Happy and You Know It")*

A circle is a shape that goes round.

A circle is a shape that goes round.

A circle is a shape that goes round,

And round and round.

A circle is a shape that goes round.

Tiptoe on the circle and go round.

Tiptoe on the circle and go round.

Tiptoe on the circle,

And go round and round and round.

Tiptoe on the circle and go round.

Square *(to the tune of "You Are My Sunshine")*

I am a square, a lovely square.

I have four sides; they're all the same.

I have four corners, four lovely corners.

I am a square; yes, that is my name!

Triangle *(to the tune of "Three Blind Mice")*

One, two, three; one, two, three.

Do you see? Do you see?

Up the hill and to the top,

Down the hill, and then you stop.

Straight across; tell me what have you got?

A triangle! A triangle!

Rectangle *(to the tune of "The Eensy Weensy Spider")*

A long line at the bottom,

A long line at the top,

A short line to connect each side,

A rectangle you've got!

A short line at the bottom

A short line at the top

A long line to connect each side

A rectangle you've got!

The kids had fun, we fulfilled a number of reading and writing and speaking and listening standards, and the songs and chants got us up out of our seats so our brains would get plenty of oxygen. I also used songs and chants as a repetitive routine every day to reinforce language skills, especially those of my ESL students. Finally, my students performed songs and chants for the community, and this was an important way to develop their confidence, attract parents to the school, and reinforce the rhythms of language.

14 Musical Reads

It is so important to get students up and out of their seats throughout the day. This is especially true with young students, so I always tried to think of ways to incorporate movement with reading. One of the games my students and I played was called "Musical Reads."

Musical Reads is basically musical chairs, except when the music stops and students sit in their chairs, they find they have a piece of writing to read. I generally used short excerpts from newspapers, brochures, junk mail, advertisement flyers, and school memos. I wanted to expose my students to lots of different writing styles, but my favorite reading materials were poems.

I think poetry is horribly underutilized in schools. Poems expose students to different cultures, writing formats, rhythms, and a variety of other things. One of the added twists I gave my students when we played "Musical Poetry" was that if they could not find a seat, a seat was added if they recited their poem aloud to the class. Just to make sure I had no little ones with hurt feelings, I used to also let students return to the game if they could recite any poem or nursery rhyme from memory.

Another way you can play the game with larger groups of students is to get rid of seats altogether and divide the group in half. Have an "inside" circle walking clockwise and an "outside" circle walking counterclockwise. When the music stops, each student should be facing another in the opposite circle; they exchange poems with their new partner, and each reads aloud her partner's poem.

15 Beanie Baby Babble

Begin telling the class a story, and when you come to a critical point, stop. Take a Beanie Baby and toss it to a student. Now the student with the Beanie Baby has to continue telling the story and toss the Beanie Baby to another student at a critical point.

This game can be modified in a number of ways. Sometimes I would require students to produce at least three new actions or add new elements in their continuation of the story. Sometimes every student had to tell the story until they added a story element, like a new character or setting. Sometimes the class and I would decide on a word for the day, and every student who caught the Beanie Baby would have to use that word in his portion of the story. If you really want to involve students, ask them all to stand up and spin around whenever the word of the day is uttered during the story. You can even pass around the Beanie Baby so that students can discuss different feelings they may have about a story or describe times in their lives when they have faced similar situations as the characters in a story.

We also used our Beanie Baby for "Traveling Stanley" projects: friends of mine and my students' parents would take photos of our classroom Beanie Baby traveling all across America and the world. The students would write stories about the Beanie Baby's adventures and make predictions about where he would wind up next.

QUICKIE STRATEGY: HOP SPELLING

One way to improve students' spelling is to place letters on the ground and allow students to "hop-spell" by hopping on different letters to spell out words. The physical movement helps students remember correct spellings and especially appeals to your kinesthetic learners.

Reference List

Allington, R.L. 2005. *What really matters for struggling readers: Designing research-based programs.* (2nd ed.) New York: Longman.

Anderson, R., Hiebert, E., Scott, J., and Wilkinson, I. 1985. *Becoming a nation of readers.* Washington, DC: U.S. Department of Education, p. 23.

Asher, James J. 2003. *Learning another language through actions (6th ed.).* Los Gatos, CA: Sky Oaks Productions, Inc.

Barr, R., and Johnson, B. 1997. *Teaching reading and writing in elementary classrooms* (2nd ed.). New York: Longman.

Blachowicz, C., and Fisher, P. J. 2002. *Teaching vocabulary in all classrooms* (2nd ed.). Upper Saddle River, NJ: Merrill/Prentice Hall.

Brassell, D. 2006. *Readers for life: The ultimate reading fitness guide, grades K–8.* Portsmouth, NH: Heinemann.

———. 2007. *News flash! Newspaper activities to meet language-arts standards & differentiate instruction.* Peterborough, NH: Crystal Springs Books.

———. 2008. *Dare to differentiate: Vocabulary strategies for all students* (2nd ed.). San Diego, CA: Academic Professional Development.

Brassell, D., and Rasinski, T. 2008. *Comprehension that works: Taking students beyond ordinary understanding to deep comprehension.* Huntington Beach, CA: Shell Education.

Cunningham, A.E., and Stanovich, K.E. 1998. "What reading does for the mind." *American Educator, 22* (1 & 2), 8–15.

———. 2003. "Reading can make you smarter!" *Principal, 83,* 34–39.

———. 2003. "Reading matters: How reading engagement influences cognition." In J. Flood, D. Lapp, J. Squire, & J. Jensen (Eds.), *Handbook of research on teaching the English language arts* (2nd ed.), pp. 666–675. Mahwah, NJ: Lawrence Erlbaum Associates.

Cunningham, P.M., and Allington, R.L. 2006. *Classrooms that work: They can all read and write* (4th ed.). Boston: Allyn & Bacon.

Feder, J. 1997. *Table, chair, bear: A book in many languages.* New York: Sandpiper Books.

Fernando, C. 1996. *Idioms and idiomaticity.* Oxford, UK: Oxford University Press.

Fountas, I., and Pinnell, G. 1996. *Guided reading: Good first teaching for all children.* Portsmouth, NH: Heinemann.

Fry, E., Kress, J., and Fountoukidis, D.L. 2000. *The reading teacher's book of lists* (4th ed.). Englewood Cliffs, NJ: Prentice-Hall.

Godin, S. 2003. *Purple cow: Transform your business by being remarkable.* New York: Portfolio Hardcover.

Graves, M.F., Juel, C., and Graves, B.B. 2006. *Teaching reading in the 21st century* (4th ed.). Boston: Allyn & Bacon.

Gruwell, E. 1999. *The freedom writers' diary.* New York: Main Street Books.

Guthrie, J.T., Gambrell, L.B., and Mandel Morrow, L. 2007. *Best practices in literacy instruction* (3rd ed.). New York: Guilford.

Halle, T.G., Kurtz-Costes, B., and Mahoney, J.L. 1997. Family influences on school achievement in low-income, African American children. *Journal of Educational Psychology, 89,* 527–537.

Hart, B., and Risley, T.R. 1995. *Meaningful differences in the everyday experience of young American children.* Baltimore, MD: Brookes.

Iversen, A.C., and Holsen, I. 2008. Inequality in health, psychosocial resources and health behavior in early adolescence: The influence of different indicators of socioeconomic position. *Child Indicators Research, 1* (3), 291–302.

Ivey, G., and Fisher, D. 2006. *Creating literacy-rich schools for adolescents.* Alexandria, VA: Association for Supervision and Curriculum Development.

Johnson, P. 2006. *One child at a time: Making the most of your time with struggling readers.* Portland, ME: Stenhouse.

Krashen, S. 2004. *The power of reading: Insights from the research* (2nd ed.). Portsmouth, NH: Heinemann.

Masterson Elementary Students. 2002. *September 12th: We knew everything would be all right.* New York: Tangerine Press.

Morrow, L.M., Dougherty Stahl, K.A., and McKenna, M.C. 2006. *Reading research at work: Foundations of effective practice.* New York: Guilford.

Nagy, W. E. 1988. *Teaching vocabulary to improve reading comprehension.* Newark, DE: International Reading Association.

National Endowment for the Arts. 2007, November. *To read or not to read: A question of national consequence.* Available: www.infoplease. com/entertainment/books/average-test-scores-number-household.html

Neuman, S. 2002. *What research reveals.* Washington, DC: U.S. Department of Education.

Ogle, D. 1986. K-W-L group instruction strategy. In A. S. Palincsar, D. S. Ogle, B. F. Jones, and E. G. Carr (Eds.), *Teaching reading as thinking.* Alexandria, VA: Association for Supervision and Curriculum Development.

———. 1992. KWL in action: Secondary teachers find applications that work. In E. K. Dishner, T. W. Bean, J. E. Readence, and D. W. Moore (Eds.), *Reading in the content areas: Improving classroom instruction* (3rd ed.). Dubuque, IA: Kendall/Hunt.

Pinnell, G.S., and Scharer, P. (Eds.) 2003. *Teaching for comprehension in reading, grades K–2.* New York: Scholastic.

Rasinski, T.V. 2003. *The fluent reader: Oral reading strategies for building word recognition, fluency, and comprehension.* New York: Scholastic.

Rasinski, T., and Padak, N. 2004. *Effective reading strategies: Teaching children who find reading difficult* (3rd ed.). Upper Saddle River, NJ: Pearson.

Rosenfeld, A., and Wise, N. 2001. *The over-scheduled child: Avoiding the hyper-parenting trap.* New York: St. Martin's Press.

Trelease, J. 2006. *The read-aloud handbook* (6th ed.). New York: Penguin.

Vacca, R.T., and Vacca, J.A.L. 2007. *Content area reading: Literacy and learning across the curriculum* (9th ed.). Boston, MA: Allyn & Bacon.

Useful Web Sites

Please note that Web sites are constantly changing, and while some may improve, others may prove less useful or become obsolete. Also, I make it a point to only refer teachers to Web sites that are free.

Here are some portal sites that I have found useful to teachers for lesson plans and work sheet templates. (I do not usually use work sheets, but they often give me ideas for fun activities I can create for my students.)

www.4teachers.org

www.about.com/education

www.altavista.com (If you have a lot of ESL students and do not speak their home language, try using a free translation tool on any search engine when creating parent communications, e.g., Alta Vista's Babel Fish.)

www.aolatschool.com

www.buildingrainbows.com/CA/ca.home.php (lesson plans broken down by grade)

www.canteach.ca (Canadian site; many English-speaking countries offer useful tools that can prove particularly helpful in differentiating instruction.)

www.edhelper.com (plenty of freebies, with a nominal fee— around $30/year for the best features)

www.edselect.com

www.education-world.com

www.educationindex.com

www.esl-lounge.com (very useful starting point for teachers of English language learners; even if you don't teach ESL students, the lessons prove helpful for differentiation.)

www.hubbardscupboard.com (wonderful kindergarten teacher personal site)

www.kinderart.com (arts-based lesson plans)

www.lessonplanspage.com

www.lessonplanz.com

www.marcopolo-education.org

www.teach-nology.com (shows how to integrate technology into curricular lessons)

www.teachercreated.com

www.teachervision.com

www.teachingheart.net/ (another great personal site by a teacher)

www.teachnet.com

www.thegateway.com

www.thesmartiezone.com

Here are some more cool sites for teachers (with brief descriptions of each site):

www.answers.com (answers to tons of questions)

www.cited.org (Center for Implementing Technology in Education; free resources for educators)

www.dominguezonline.csudh.edu (CSUDH offers several free online courses.)

www.ed.gov/free/index.html (free materials for teachers)

www.eduref.org (online teacher encyclopedia)

http://edweb.sdsu.edu/courses/edtec670/Cardboard/Matrix.html (awesome games with accompanying standards-based lesson plans)

www.internet4classrooms.com (great reproducibles, e.g., certificates and flashcards)

www.kididdles.com/mouseum/ (full-text songs, nursery rhymes, and lullabies)

www.mothergoose.com (Mother Goose nursery rhymes)

http://ocw.mit.edu (MIT OpenCourseWare allows you free access to MIT courses.)

www.reacheverychild.com (teacher resource links)

www.readingrockets.org (parent resources, recommended reading lists)

www.refdesk.com (one of the best online encyclopedias)

http://searchlight.utexas.org (free teacher professional development resources)

www.sitesforteachers.com/ (shows most popular sites for teachers)

www.stepstoliteracy.com (teacher supply store with material ideas)

www.webring.com/hub?ring=teachersnet (teacher's links to favorite K–12 sites)

www.webring.com/hub?ring=teachkids (teacher's links to favorite elementary sites)

Here are some Web sites for teachers that deal specifically with literacy-related activities (with brief descriptions of each site):

www.acs.ucalgary.ca/~dkbrown (great children's literature Web guide)

www.ala.org (American Library Association; lots of great recommended reading lists) www.alphadictionary.com/ww/goodwordjr/ (great vocabulary games)

www.bookends.org (literacy nonprofit)

www.carolhurst.com (children's literature site with book reviews and professional resources)

www.cbcbooks.org (Children's Book Council; more recommended reading lists)
www.edsitement.neh.gov (National Endowment for the Humanities; lesson plans and Web links)

www.eduscapes.com/ladders/ (awesome links to materials for Caldecott and Newbery winners)

www.funbrain.com/idioms (kid games for learning idioms)

www.gigglepoetry.com (filled with all sorts of funny poems)

www.guysread.com (recommended books for boys; sponsored by children's author Jon Scieszka)

www.hanswilhelm.com (Hans has placed the full text *and pictures* of over 100 of his out-of-print books on this site.)

www.janbrett.com (wonderful author site with useful teacher links)

www.justriddlesandmore.com (riddles and jokes)

www.kids.mysterynet.com (kid mysteries)

www.lexile.com (shows readability level of texts)

www.readwritethink.org (expert-reviewed lessons)

www.rif.org (Reading Is Fundamental; national literacy nonprofit with recommended reading lists)

www.us.penguingroup.com (*Mad Libs!*)

Here are some Web sites for teachers that boost many students' reading by providing activities in math and logic (with brief descriptions of each site):

www.aimsedu.org/puzzle/index.html (puzzles)

www.aplusmath.com (downloadable flashcards)

www.c3.lanl.gov/mega-math/ (math activities)

www.enchantedmind.com (puzzles and tangrams)

www.funbrain.com/cashreg (money conversion game)

www.greylabyrinth.com (puzzles)

www.illuminations.nctm.org/ (expert-reviewed lessons)

www.learner.org/teacherslab (math games)

www.library.rider.edu/scholarly/rlackie/sci/ (math and science explained for lay people)

www.mape.org.uk/activities (great sorting games, e.g., fairy tales)

http://nlvm.usu.edu/en/nav/vlibrary.html (math sorting games)

www.themoneymammals.com (economics for kids)

Here are some Web sites for teachers that boost many students' reading by providing activities in science and social studies (with brief descriptions of each site):

http://amazing-space.stsci.edu/eds/tools/ (science resources)

www.congress.org (updates on legislation; write Congressional officials)

www.digitalhistory.uh.edu (history from multiple perspectives)

www.econedlink.org/ (great civics site)

www.education.jlab.org (science lessons; reviewed by teachers and kids)

www.eyewitnesstohistory.com (sort of like Edward R. Murrow's show *You Were There*)

www.funbrain.com/who (great game—match inventor with what s/he invented)

www.games.funschool.com (science matching games)

www.mapquest.com (maps and directions)

www.nationalatlas.gov (atlas of the United States)

www.nationalgeographic.com/xpeditions (Indiana Jones-like adventures for kids)

www.nsdl.org (National Science Digital Library; science lessons)

www.ology.amnh.org (science taught by passionate experts)

www.quest.nasa.gov/about/ (NASA)

www.sheppardsoftware.com (game in which students place states in correct place on map)

www.usacitylink.com (information about cities in America)

www.weather.com/ (weather maps)

Here are some more cool sites for students (with brief descriptions of each site):

www.ajkids.com (kid search engine: kid-friendly sites)

www.factmonster.com (kid search engine: kid-friendly sites)

www.kidinfo.com/ (homework help)

www.storylineonline.net (audio Web site that features celebrities reading aloud popular children's books; sponsored by BookPals and SAG)

www.sunsite.berkeley.edu/KidsClick! (kid search engine: kid-friendly sites)

www.webquest.org (WebQuests are Internet-integrated assignments that require students to use online resources to solve a problem that is presented in a role-playing scenario.)

www.yahooligans.com (kid search engine: kid-friendly sites)

Here are 10 of my favorite Web sites for teachers. Trust me— you'll be glad you checked out these sites.

www.discoveryschool.com

www.iris.peabody.vanderbilt.edu

www.lazyreaders.com

www.pbskids.org

www.professorgarfield.org

www.scholastic.com

www.starfall.com

www.techtrekers.com

www.ted.com

www.trelease-on-reading.com

Here are some other useful Web sites presented in the order they were mentioned in the text. Realize that the Internet is dynamic and many of these sites may have changed (especially anything that appears on YouTube).

www.teachertube.com (sample lessons)

http://youtube.com/watch?v=GES3um1HYcM (interesting statistics)

www.artsedge.kennedy-center.org (The Kennedy Center)

www.metmuseum.org/ (The Metropolitan Museum of Art)

www.playmusic.org (teaches students about the instruments found in an orchestra)

www.americanrhetoric.com (famous speeches)

www.madlibs.com (home of *Mad Libs!*)

www.puzzlemaker.com (free word finds)

Index

Also by Danny Brassell

A Baker's Dozen of Lessons Learned from the Teacher's Trenches

Comprehension That Works: Taking Students Beyond Ordinary Understanding to Deep Comprehension, K–6

Dare to Differentiate: Vocabulary Strategies for All Students

News Flash! Newspaper Activities to Meet Language-Arts Standards & Differentiate Instruction

Readers for Life: The Ultimate Reading Fitness Guide, K–8

Vocabulary Strategies Every Teacher Needs to Know